KT-590-073

CLXX

49

BOOK NO   **0910625**

30109 0 09106256

THE SWAN'S ROAD

East of the Sun, west of the Moon

THE
SWAN'S ROAD

by

NAOMI MITCHISON

CLXX

With drawings by
LEONARD HUSKINSON

The Naldrett Press

First published 1954
by the Naldrett Press Ltd
98 Great Russell Street
London, WC1

★

A11311

(V 8514)
F

VNF 1633

948·02
MIT

51

Made and printed in Great Britain by
WILLIAM CLOWES AND SONS, LIMITED, LONDON AND BECCLES,
and set in Monotype Bembo

CONTENTS

ILLUSTRATIONS

Illustrations by LEONARD HUSKINSON

Books by the same author

The Conquered
Cloud Cuckoo Land
Black Sparta
The Corn King and the Spring Queen
An Outline for Boys and Girls and their Parents
The Delicate Fire
We Have Been Warned
The Moral Basis of Politics
The Fourth Pig
The Blood of the Martyrs
The Bull Calves
Lobsters on the Agenda
Travel Light

DRAGONS

THIS BOOK is about the people who came from the other side of the North Sea from us. It is about the sea and the edges of the sea, where, in fjords and sea-lochs and creeks, ships and wild swans can shelter, taking to the seaways when times are favourable for them.

Wherever swans went they left a shape of beauty in men's minds. They became sacred and magic birds, unlucky to kill, since they might be a shape taken by gods or water-maids or king's children under a spell. Stories and songs were made around them and still are. They built nests of sticks and rushes on the tide edge and hatched their eggs, and in time the sticks of the nest would be broken and dispersed by winds and storms.

But it was otherwise with the men who came over from the places where the ships sheltered. The signs of their coming were children, place-names and a great many ideas and habits and ways of doing things which we have inherited from them. Most of us in this vulnerable island of Great Britain have Norse ancestors if we go back far enough, especially if we come from the north-east coast of England, the north or east of Scotland, the Orkneys, the Shetlands or the Hebrides. When we look at the map, we see hundreds – thousands if it is a big enough scale – of names of towns and places which end in '-by', or '- wick', or '-ham', or '-dale', or '-thorpe', or '-ness' or '-garth'. These names were given by Danish or Norwegian people who crossed the sea, sometimes as raiders and conquerors, sometimes more peaceably, but always in sail-winged ships by the Swan's Road.

When one begins to think about all this, the whole thing opens out into a series of questions. This book is my attempt to answer these questions – why did they come, how is it they were among our ancestors, what sort of people were they and how do their ideas and their ways of life link up with ours? I am inclined to think that some of these questions are best answered indirectly. This is the kind of thing they said of themselves: it tells us how they liked to be thought of – how does it strike us, their descendants? If it provokes a sympathetic response, then we and they are that much alike. That is why I have gone into detail about some of the people and have sometimes put in, not necessarily what is historically true, but what they would like one to have thought. This seems to me to be the properly sympathetic treatment from one imaginative writer to another, across the centuries which need not divide us.

The first question, of course, is why did they come, what made them leave their homes? Now, people who live along the edge of any civilisation are always finding reasons for going a little farther. Many of these are trade reasons, and trade may turn in the end into wars of invasion and conquest. There was certainly a little trading across the Swan's Road before the main movement began, in fact we can trace it back for an astonishing number of centuries. But before it could be enlarged there had to be enough sea-going ships and experienced men to sail in them. That came gradually, though, as always with this kind of thing, there seems to have been a crisis time when everything was ready and, quite quickly, a new historical stage became recognisable.

Traders, too, will bring back stories, and these will lead to action of another kind. But there was no deliberate opening up of markets and trade routes, of the type which became familiar to Europeans from the fifteenth to the early twentieth centuries. Nor was there pure curiosity or even scientific concern, the modern excuse for travel, though there is some evidence that the men who came in the ships were the kind of people who always longed to know just exactly what was round the corner.

They did not go on shipboard to spread their religion or way of life, as so many of their descendants have done. They had not got sufficiently outside themselves to see this as a reason for leaving home. Nor did they, at any rate at the beginning, go to escape from any kind of persecution.

But we do know that this move overseas started through certain conditions in the Norse homeland and was made possible by the Norse timber from which the ships were built and by the seamanship which people who live along a coast must have in order to survive. Archaeologists and historians on both sides of the North Sea have made it their business to find out as far as possible what the conditions were which started the move. That must be checked against what the people themselves gave as their reasons in their poems and stories. It appears that about fifteen hundred years ago, more or less the same kind of people were living in Norway, southern Sweden and Denmark. For the sake of simplicity we can call them all Norsemen. We know that, although they spoke different dialects, they could understand one another. They wore the same kind of clothes and had the same kind of weapons, though, of course, there were always small local differences. Their kings and kinglets were related. They had the same way of life and the same standards of good and bad conduct. And there was constant coming and going across the narrow seas between them. For the Norsemen, the Viking folk, just as for the ancient Greeks, the sea was not a boundary, but a road: the Swan's Road they called it, and indeed they had many names for it, since it was the great inducer of excitement and poetry.

These people prospered. The population grew. But all the arable land was cultivated and they knew no scientific ways of increasing the yield of barley, oats and rye, and of making their cows give more milk. When the land was divided up among the sons the holdings became unworkably small. The same thing happens all over the world where farmers and peasants want big families so as to have plenty of unpaid help on the land and then have to divide. Sooner or later the nature of cultivation asserts itself and the broken landholdings have to be put together by one method or another.

Norway is mountainous anyhow, and most people lived near the sea where the river valleys broadened out a little so that they could grow crops and catch fish, to eat fresh or to salt for winter. They clustered together in harbour villages round the big wooden house of the main landholder, the earl or little king. The way out, to plenty, to food and drink and fine clothes, was over the sea. Denmark has no mountains and plenty of level land. But in order to make it fertile, it needed draining and clearing. Acres of heathland are still being brought into cultivation in Denmark today. There was pressure of growing population there too.

As the Swan's Road opened and became more attractive it was plain to everyone that a ship was more valuable than a bit of land. So the eldest son took the ship and the noble life of the fighting man. The younger ones took the holding and the comparatively despised life of the cultivator. This inheritance of land by the younger son was the basis of the tenure called Borough English which still existed in parts of the old Danish settlements in England until the last legal tidying up.

It is a queer thing how words change their meaning – that is, their whole meaning including emotions centred round them. 'Land' is one of these words which has been emotionally potent in feudal or ex-feudal societies where land-holding was power.

Not so long ago people talked of the British Empire as the 'land on which the sun never sets' or 'land of hope and glory'. At the same time the Germans were talking about *lebensraum* – room to live. One has only to think of all the national anthems with the word 'land' in them. We would feel it inappropriate if they substituted 'credit' or 'hydro-electric power' or even 'fertility'. One has also to think of all the people who have been caught by the romantic associations of the word and have run themselves into trouble with hens or tomatoes just because they have the feeling that landowning is something which almost magically assures success. It will be quite a long time before we get out of this feudal feeling about land.

But the first Norse people were pre-feudal. They thought realistically about land and all the hard work attached to it, for they were not slave-owners in a big way; they had to do a great deal of the land work themselves. What stirred them was gold. Gold was something which got you everything the land got you and more, but without having to work. Gold was a fairy thing, a witch thing, that you wanted not only realistically for its exchange value but romantically for itself. It was the eldest son's thing, the guerdon of the ship and the sword and it had power of its own. It could pull people for better or worse. Gold comes over and over into the earliest poems and stories.

Ordinary currency in so far as it existed was very largely silver. But you didn't think of gold simply as coin, to buy other things with, still less to stick into Fort Knox, where most of the world's gold goes now, but to give away in handfuls. A great king was always a gold-giver. His greatness was measured by his generosity. In those days you wore gold on your arms and neck for pride and delight, and to be nearer the gods. The first travellers and explorers were looking for gold, for the fairy source of it perhaps, the land where it was as common as stones. For it did tend even then, just as gold does now, to disappear into bank vaults. These were, of course, natural caves, and the bankers, who curled themselves up, smoking over the gold, were dragons. It was well known, especially to poets, whose opinions were respected in those days, that dragons liked gold. They collected treasure, not to display it on board or breast, but simply to hoard it in the unlighted dark. This was not to be borne. The hero must journey, dragon slayer and banker slayer.

Somewhere back in the beginnings of Norse history, Beowulf, the younger son of the king of South Sweden, crossed the narrow seas to Denmark to kill the man-eating Grendel, the shadow walker, striding the wan light. He did it the heroic way, without sword or shield, but with sure handgrip, life for life and hate for hate. Then he hunted the monstrous mother of Grendel through 'wolf slopes, windy nesses, paths of risk between bogs where mountain streams go sliding, dropping down the headlands under mist', and killed her in the bottom of a terrible mere. Later he himself became king and guarded his people. He was an old man when an angry dragon began to come out at nights ravaging and burning. Beowulf had to find its cave and kill it, but his sword was turned on the dragon's bone and he was terribly scorched by its breath and his neck was bitten. A young kinsman came to his help and between them they managed to kill the dragon, but Beowulf was wounded to death. He saw the dragon's hoard, gold cups and gems, helmets and bracelets, dead men's gold; and the dragon 'fifty measured feet long' dead at last. So Beowulf died and his people buried him in a great mound with the dragon's treasure round him, as it is written in the poem which was made by an Anglo-Saxon about A D 700.

It is, of course, open to anyone to say that this is all nonsense. There were no dragons. If there had been dragons we would have found their bones. The descriptions of dragons correspond with no possible animal. Poets are certainly not to be trusted, and the early chroniclers who wrote about dragons were not much better than poets.

That may well be so, but all the same there is an odd connection between gold and dragons. If the dragons were not real, why were they invented? What were they symbols for? If they were symbols, why were these symbols used? How do dragons compare with some of the symbols which are used by modern economists?

Again, did some poet start it off and the rest follow? Did everyone who got away with a successful robbery agree to say he had vanquished a dragon? Or, if people then thought they were real, ought not we, if we are trying to see what those people were really like, to assume some kind of reality for dragons or anything else of the same kind? That may lead us into some rather curious places. Perhaps we ought simply to say there were no dragons and leave it at that. But then, what was there which induced people to make up dragon stories? History begins with asking questions.

What we do know is that many of these early explorers and adventurers were, just the same as Beowulf, the sons of noble and kingly families, though one must always remember that the kingdom might be tiny and the king merely the leader who was chosen by the others for his courage and intelligence. They had to set off (like the surplus third son in the fairy-tales) to seek their fortunes and find treasures. They would bring as many of their friends as would come with them. And the easiest way to go, in the days when in northern Europe outwith the boundaries of the old Roman Empire the best roads were no more than pack-horse trails, was by ship in the calm summer days, over the Swan's Road.

In Great Britain, of course, we see it from the other end. When the treasure-seekers in the eighth and ninth centuries came to Christian England, Scotland or Ireland, they sacked the churches and houses of people whose civilisation very often went back either to the greatness of Rome or to the learning and poetry of the Celtic courts and bards. It may have been that the raiders described dragons when they went home. Some at least, like Beowulf in the old poem, were buried with their golden treasure round them.

These raiders were the people known as Vikings. Perhaps they were called that because they came from and sheltered in the viks or creeks. They were out for what they could get and expected to have to fight for it. But in those days a stranger must be prepared to have stones thrown at him. He must either fight or be fought. The boundary line between traveller, explorer and raider is not very clear. But there is one Norse traveller who went on his way before all the others and was doubtless in all their minds, even after his name was forbidden to their tongues. Odin, the oldest and chief of the Norse gods, was called the Wanderer.

When other gods stayed serenely and suitably in their heaven, and when indeed the rest of the Aesir, the gods and goddesses of Asgaard, sat at their age-long feasts behind the rainbow-girdled walls of Valhalla, Odin, the All-Father, went wandering in his blue cloak and hat, disguised as an old one-eyed beggar-man or story-teller. Sometimes he went on foot with his ravens, Hugin and Munin, the scythe-eyed birds of council, and sometimes he would hurry from place to place on his six-legged horse, Sleipnir. He would walk in and out of people's houses, leaving here a curse and there a blessing, runes of warning and doom, or a magic sword, disconcertingly planted in the middle of the living-room, to be drawn only by the fated hero. In so far as we are descended from Odin's folk, he is perhaps the wanderer in our minds.

THE WORLD BEYOND

THESE Norse boats were well built, and we are lucky to be able to see them with our own eyes, as we can, for instance, in the open-air museum at Oslo. A man who owned and loved a ship, and had lived in and with and for her most of his days, would be buried in her, with most of his own things, which were not thought of apart from him – his tent and bed, which used to go on shipboard on a long voyage; his hounds and oxen and any pet animals he might have; his carved wagon and the horses that drew it; his drinking horn and dishes, perhaps a great cooking-pot; his shirts and cloaks and bracelets, his war-shirt of linked metal, which might have a name of its own, his axe and spear; above all the sword that was always by his side, that was usually named, whose blade sang to him, and whose hilt, wrought with gold and enamel and mountain stones, was sure grip to his hand's hollow. And all would be piled with earth into a great cairn; and the flesh would pass, but the bone and iron and much of the wood remained.

There is a singularly horrible description of a Norse funeral* in one

* A translation (from a Danish version) was published in the *Proceedings of the Society of Antiquaries of Scotland*, Vol. IX.

of the Russian city-states where there was a large Varangian community, written by an Arab called Ahmed Ibn-Fozlan; he was an
ambassador of the tenth-century Caliph Al-Moktader. The caliph's
court must have been one of the most civilised places in the world at
that time. Ahmed Ibn-Fozlan, like a modern civilised person, found the
whole thing shocking but interesting. In this burial the ship had been
drawn up on to the beach – probably of the Volga – and raised on
posts, and the whole thing was burnt. Ibn-Fozlan says that even a poor
man is burnt on a boat. The whole description is of a somewhat
different culture from that of the chief who was buried in the Gokstad
ship, but no doubt something of the same kind happened there; one
can assume a certain conservatism about funeral rites. In this burial the
richly dressed body was laid on a bed with gold-embroidered pillows
in the ship; food and drink was put in with the body, and also a harp,
perhaps like the little harp from the Sutton Hoo grave which is in the
British Museum. His dog and pack horses, oxen and poultry were all
killed. A tent was set up over all.

But what most interested and shocked Ibn-Fozlan was the death of
a slave girl, who had offered to die with him. Sometimes a wife would
do this, killing herself on the pyre as Brynhild does with Siegfried.
This girl was taken charge of by a 'sallow and stern' woman known
as the dead man's angel and given much strong drink. She was lifted
up on to a kind of frame like a trilithion, where she sacrificed a hen
and spoke of the dead whom she saw, last of all crying out 'Lo, here I
see my master seated in Paradise – Paradise beautiful and green ! My
master surrounded by his men and slaves ! He calls me: bring me to
him.'

She now drank and sang and climbed on to the ship, still singing.
'I saw her; she was out of herself.' The dead man's angel pulled her
into the tent while the men beat their shields with their spears. She
was now laid on the marriage bed with the dead man, a cord pulled
round her neck and a knife stabbed between her ribs. Then the dead
man's nearest relation set light to the pyre and all was burnt. Afterwards they threw up a grave mound over the ashes and set up a birch
trunk on which they carved the name of the dead man and his king –
no doubt in runes.

If there was a funeral like that, whether the dead man was burnt or
buried, the mound would become a terrifying and haunted place. For
a long time people would be too frightened of ghosts to dig into the
mound and disturb it, even though the tale of the riches buried with

2*

the dead might grow from year to year. There are a good many stories in the sagas of daring men who went into grave mounds and conversed with ghosts. Angantyr's daughter went into his grave mound and took his sword for herself and her own vengeance. The dead might be terribly strong and hostile.

But other civilisations came with their own fears and their own greeds; they broke into many of the grave mounds, and stole and scattered the dead men's gear. In our own time a very few of these burials which still remained untouched have been dug up with loving care; objects which were likely to crumble away when after so many centuries the air got at them, were photographed during the few hours when they still held their shape. Some could be restored. And in this way we can still see the actual ship of the ship burial, so well designed with its grand sea-going lines and its high prow.

It is clear at once how like they are to the modern Scandinavian and Shetland inshore boats. They are built by the same kind of people for the same kind of seas and out of the same kind of wood. But those we see are not in any sense primitive boats. There were many hundreds of years of practice in boat building behind them since the first hide-and-wicker coracles of the Bronze Age.

They had rowers, of course, as well as sails, but these rowers were free men and fighters. This was different from the Mediterranean galley, where there were probably several tiers of oarsmen, four or five to the oar, rowing in slum conditions. In war service, the oarsmen, in the Greek and Byzantine navies, tended on the whole to be non-citizens, free or freedmen, but so long as there were plenty of cheap slaves, it would be usual to use slave labour in merchant ships. In times of stress they would certainly be used in war-ships too. But the Mediterranean ship was specialised. The oarsmen just rowed, like machines, and under a hard discipline. The Norse rowers were the crew, and the captain would be at the heavy steering oar; the discipline was what they made for themselves.

Except with a very favourable wind a Norse long-ship would sail a good deal slower than a modern fishing-boat: it might take them weeks to cross the North Sea, though if they were lucky it might be four or five days. The imitation Viking ship, the *Hugin*, crossed the North Sea with sail and oar in nine days, in July 1949. Sometimes they would be blown out of their course, and if there were a heavy fog, especially if the wind shifted when they were still in it, they might actually be lost. They had no compasses: probably the first compass, a

The professor and the long serpent

lodestone balanced on a straw in a bowl of water, was brought north not more than a thousand years ago, perhaps later than that. (The description of the compass in Kipling's 'Knights of the Joyous Venture' in *Puck of Pook's Hill* is probably very like the real thing and how it happened.) They had very little in the way of charts, though no doubt they got to know their marks well, as inshore fishermen do nowadays, and had plenty of sea-knowledge handed down about tides and currents.

I think it is worth considering what people's ideas about geography were a thousand years ago. We are used to accurate maps. We have a rough idea of the world, though I think we sometimes get a wrong idea through the use of old-fashioned projections which make Iceland look larger than India. Because all the maps I learnt from had the north at the top of the page, I always find myself thinking of anywhere from the south, which always means a most annoying mental jump when I get to the real thing. But it is not only that. Most of us have walked or cycled with quarter-inch and half-inch scale maps, but if we didn't have them, we would have to depend on the sun and our own ideas of distance, depending very much on how tired we were, whether the road went a little uphill or a little downhill, and so on. In hill country, where the roads twist and turn, we would lose our direction very quickly, as anyone knows who has tried to make a sketch map for someone else. Possibly these Norsemen would have the kind of detailed knowledge which is more of a 'feel' than anything else about their own fjords and the countryside for ten miles round. But beyond that, distances and directions would get increasingly inaccurate, and once you get inaccuracies about the basic facts of geography, you are very likely to get dragons and unipeds, centaurs and dog-headed men and every kind of queer thing. It is possible that some of the Norsemen may have seen copies of the maps of the world which were made by Greek and Roman geographers and which all started from a fairly well-known Mediterranean, but this kind of map must have seemed fantastic and unpractical to people who lived so far from the middle, so near to what the geographers called Ultima Thule. After all, we are all in the middle of our own map !

None of this map-making would have been any use to the man in the sailing ship who had gone out beyond the mouth of his own fjord and beyond the immediate capes and landmarks which he knew. Many ships must have been lost and many good men with them. And sometimes one of these adventurous skippers would go as far as any man had gone before and then beyond that, and he would see on a fair day fantastic peaks in a pale sky, and what was behind them beyond his knowledge, maybe beyond mortal knowledge. For it seemed to the Norsemen that the far north was the home of the giants: Jotunheim, full of the crashings and roarings and the knockings and squeakings like giant puppies, that now we think come from the moving pack-ice or icebergs knocking against cliffs, and whose nights throb with the stabbing, wavering northern lights, very beautiful, but also very menacing, even to ourselves. Who knew what would happen to a man if he came too close to giants or gods?

We know about one of those skippers. This was Ottar, the Nor-wegian, who talked to our own King Alfred about his voyage in the days when that very remarkable man was translating and bringing up to date the books of Orosius, which were the main text-books of his time for history and geography. King Alfred wanted to know what happened in the far north, beyond known geography, and he wrote down in a very straightforward way just what Ottar told him. In the Anglo-Saxon narrative Ottar is called Ohthere – he is there again in Longfellow's poem. He explained how he lived in the far north of Norway, with nobody beyond him but the Finns and Lapps, who wandered about hunting in winter and sea-fishing in summer and were well known as magicians. He was a very rich man in the wealth of his own country, that was to say mostly in reindeer, including six decoy reindeer which were used for catching the wild ones, and the Finns gave him tribute of skins and eider-down.

Ottar was a genuine explorer in the sense that he wanted to know what there was round the corner, and it was round the corner he went: the very farthest corner, the North Cape. Once round the corner he turned south-east and explored along the coast rather timorously, because the country was inhabited and if he had landed he would probably have been attacked. There was something very valuable along these shores, something which was already known and might be the worthiest part of a gift from one king to another. This valuable com-modity was the walrus, whose ivory tusks were only a little smaller and less white than elephant ivory and whose hide made tremendously durable thongs. The Norwegian and his crew killed sixty of them and brought back their tusks, some of which he gave to King Alfred. No doubt they were made good use of: given out to skilled Saxon carvers and engravers to make such things as caskets, cups, the crook of a bishop's crozier or a set of chess-men.

We must remember, I think, that one of the main objects of extending the borders of knowledge, whether in geography or medicine or any other science or half-science, was and perhaps still is that it pushes back the barriers of the unknown and terrifying. We are still trying to push back this same barrier, though today it seems to threaten us in other directions, from within ourselves as much as from without. In those days the threat was clearer; it was straight Death, often seen and seldom avoided for as long as we normally manage to avoid it now.

Once you left the warmth and closeness of the house and companionship of family and friends, the unknown was facing you, trolls in the mountains, dwarfs below the mountains, wild beasts that nobody had ever named. You might yourself have seen a white bear, or at least have seen the polar pelt in front of an altar or in the house of a chief. Later people saw the great white bearskin at the foot of the Archbishop's throne in Trondheim cathedral.* But surely there were worse creatures yet! Yet there might also be fairy lands, places of continual youth and feasting, golden bracelets and coronets, glimpses of an earthly paradise. From the earliest times when men's imagination began to go a little farther than they could see, there were rumours of some such paradise in the west, beyond the sunset: if a man could notch the prow of his boat evening after evening into the setting sun. Such beaches were called *furdus-strands* (wonder beaches) or Hvitramanna land (land of the white men) or the Great Strand or the Happy Plain or the Land of Maidens. Many were the stories told about such countries and many were the songs sung. Some merged with the first Utopias of hungry men, where pigs ran about ready-roasted, and there were no masters and no money. There were cauldrons of plenty, which later perhaps became grails, when the stories were given a new twist. But the way was always difficult and dangerous and if you could not guess the riddle you had to go back.

And what of the real south from which came all the beautiful man-made things with which the noble and rich adorned their houses and their families? From what hot and glorious lands came the kirtles and kerchiefs and hair bands for flax-maned maidens, of stiff and shining silk, embroidered in gold and silver and all colours, with pillared palaces, horses in chariots and long-robed people not like the people of the north? From where the cunningly made belts, the drinking cups of beaten metal, different altogether from the homely ox horn? From where the wavy patterned, well-tempered sword blades? From where the delicate pottery, smooth and light as sea shells? From where the

* But this was not actually mentioned until the fifteenth century.

dried fruit, dark and sweet and seedy, grapes and figs, dried by a sun hotter than the northern sun at mid-summer? From where the oil and the olives, the spices that made the winter stews of salted meat tasty and wholesome? And could it be true that this southern ivory, polished and white as a bowl of curds, came from no walrus or sea-beast, but from a creature like a whale, huge, but a land-goer, and with a serpent between its eyes? It would have seemed improbable to many people of the time if they were told authoritatively that an elephant was a real beast, but a dragon was not.

In the Norse picture of the south there were neither gods nor giants, but many men and women living round a tideless sea. They had great and beautiful cities of which the greatest was Constantinople, that was also called Byzantium, and that was Micklegard to the Norsemen because it was so great, so mickle! And many wonders were told of it, yet it seemed that the most unbelievable might even be true.

It was known in the dark northern halls where men sat round the fires talking and wondering that there were more ways than one to get to the south. For it was possible to go all the way in ships by the Swan's Road, south-west and so into the Middle Sea, past the Pillars of Hercules. But only a bold man would go that way, for there was a voyage of many weeks and there were rough seas to be crossed. Yet if one went by land there were a thousand land dangers. A stranger beyond the reach of his own law had only his own and his friends' swords as his defence, for a lucky traveller might come to the court of a hospitable king or noble and he might be well treated and bring back marvellous stories. But an unlucky one, or one coming at an unfortunate moment, might be thrown into a dungeon and have all his goods and gear taken from him and his life might end miserably. And a man would not be able to speak with the outlanders in their own tongue, and there might be thieves, or he might come to a town with the plague in it, or he might find himself in a land where the crops had failed and there was no food for citizen or stranger. He might be sold into slavery or he might be bewitched. And he would never reach Micklegard, still less come back from it.

But as the generations went by, the roads seemed to open up. There were wars and invasions that a bold man might take for his opportunity. It began to be possible to go by the south-east, and here where the rivers met other cities arose, almost as wonderful as Micklegard, the new trading cities of Novgorod and Kiev, where all men met in amity to buy and sell, and where all tongues were spoken, and

LABRADOR

Hudson Strait

Labrador Current

Western Settle
BRA

Cape Farewe

Cape Farewe

White Bay

NEWFOUNDLAND

NOVA SCOTIA

Cape Cod

MAP I

Broadfirth
Faxo Bay

FAROES

BERGEN

SHETLANDS

ORKNEYS

...LD
...ettlement

Gulf Stream

DUBLIN

LONDON

all foods were cooked and eaten, and all kinds of exchanges made. There was much river traffic from there, and it might be that in the end this would be the easiest way to Micklegard and the Middle Sea. But at first movement was slow and people's imagination moved gropingly towards anything new.

Meanwhile in Norway, Sweden and Denmark, the prosperous families grew more prosperous; they intermarried; they quarrelled and had blood-feuds. They developed a system of government with a kind of parliament, a formal meeting of heads of families where laws were made and enforced and matters of importance discussed. There was a general spreading outward into other countries round the Baltic, many of the families going to Esthonia and Latvia and thereabouts. The Swedes went raiding into Russia and stayed to found dynasties. Gradually farming and craftsmanship, house-building and ship-building improved, though there were no sudden changes. People still lived in great wooden-pillared halls with perhaps a bower for the women and, along the sides, big beds with shelves round them, curtained off for privacy. But even the greatest halls were more like farms than palaces. Master and man and the beasts they tended and used all slept under one roof within smell and hearing of one another, though the beasts were usually partitioned off to some extent. The days were busy and the summer days were very long whether for farming or fighting, making things, playing games, rowing, sailing or riding. But the winter days were short and the evenings ill-lighted and the storms lashing round the great halls. It was well if you had someone to tell you stories and sing you songs to pass the time.

Every family and community would have some people who were skilled in this craft of singing and telling, but there were also professional singers, the *skalds*, and the story-tellers, paid in hospitality and honour and maybe now and then a taste of the fairy gold, but on the whole landless and swordless men. And in time they began to write down the stories. Writing had come in first to commemorate words and names which were too important for mere tongue-speech. But after a time it spread from its high purpose and came to be used for such things as reckoning values and times and for the better remembering of stories.

These stories are the sagas. How lucky we are that so many of them were written down while they were still honoured! Many of our own Celtic many-night stories which were still told only two or three generations ago in the western Highlands and islands of Scotland are now irretrievably lost, just because an English culture thought little of them. A few were gathered up by Irish or Scandinavian scholars.

But the sagas never fell into real disrepute in Scandinavia. And every westerner who cares about good writing should have them as part of his cultural background. They are magnificently concise, going straight to the point; most of them are lively, some still very dramatic and moving, and all of them full of good small touches. Many have been very well translated into English, partly because the people in them are not unlike ourselves; they do things for the same kind of reason and they speak in the same kind of idiom as we do. In fact they translate much better into modern colloquial English than anything in Greek or Latin, in spite of much talk about our Greek and Roman heritage! Most of this book will be based on various sagas, and they have been a constant delight to read. In quoting from them I have sometimes altered a word or two here and there to make them run more easily, especially in the Vinland story where, even more than in the others, one feels oneself in the middle of it all.

There is a great deal to be said about the sagas, but I want only to make one or two points. Women and girls had plenty of say in the lives of most Norse communities, whether in their original home or in the places they colonised later. Women were taken seriously: they owned property; they were good (or bad) counsellors; they might join in almost any adventure. You never get the feeling in the sagas that they were looked down upon and handed round like any other bit of property, as they were in most southern European countries, not only at that time but for many centuries later. I am sure this was partly because when the men of any community go off voyaging, trading, raiding and exploring for half the year, the women have to manage things at home. This also helps to space out the families, so married women tend to be healthier and live longer. We see the same thing among the Ionian Greeks in the sixth and seventh centuries B C, where the men went off on long trading voyages, leaving the women to look after the affairs and incidentally to write poetry, as Sappho and her friends did.

Then again the heroes of the sagas are sometimes quite young. You read an account of a fierce battle in which somebody ambushes somebody else and cuts off his head. The saga then mentions, quite casually, that at the time he was twelve years old! King Olaf Tryggvasson's mother was captured by pirates and sold into slavery; he himself was only three years old at the time and was sold separately. The saga explains that he was quite well treated and finally rescued by his uncle, when he was nine. Within a few months of that, he was walking through the crowded market place of Novgorod when he saw the pirate who had sold his mother. He immediately killed him with his axe! – and was then only with difficulty rescued by Queen Alogia, since in the normal course of things anyone committing a murder within the bounds of Novgorod was himself condemned to death.

The other thing is this. These sagas are so good that while we are reading them we just don't ask ourselves whether or not they are true. We accept them because they are convincing and because they are partly about people who are known from other accounts to have really existed. On the other hand they are just as convincing about dragons, sorcerers and various other things which most people do not believe in now. I am not sure about all this myself. I have an idea that even now we may not always be right in our choice of what we think credible. Some people, for instance, do and some do not believe in the Loch Ness monster, and many people have had experiences which they are ashamed to speak about because they are not explicable in terms of respectable western science. But I am also sure that the people who made the sagas did embroider them a little just as country people are apt to embroider any story which they think will be the better for it. The saga-makers had not yet begun to think of history texts and novels as two separate kinds of things. There was always a foundation of what really happened, but they were determined to make a good story of it so that people might admire them and remember it. And that is exactly what they succeeded in doing.

GO WEST, YOUNG MAN

THE Roman Empire existed in people's minds long after it had passed and changed into something else. Once it had been all-powerful. The outer world of barbarians had broken against its boundaries manned by the Legions. Then gradually there came a shifting of the centre of power and a softening of the frontiers. The barbarians crossed the frontiers but became absorbed in the changing structure of the old civilisation. The ancient shell of history and legend was recharged with the power of the Christian religion which had two sides, one working among the mass of the people with its hope of justice and judgment and brotherhood and the other amongst those who saw in it a new kind of power.

Nobody tried to destroy the name of Rome, but rather to identify themselves with it. Charlemagne the Frank was crowned in Holy Rome and finally recognised by the Emperors of the East; they were even partly prepared to admit that he was, temporarily at least, almost their equal. He stiffened the frontiers again and terrorised the Saxons who lived between his Empire and Denmark, forcing them to choose between his variety of Christianity and death. Along his northern coast-line he had a fleet and some kind of guards, specifically against Viking attack. He took to himself what he could of the legend of Rome, and after his death still more was heaped on to him, so that he became terror and wonder and death dealer. In the year 814 he died, and his top-heavy western 'Empire' began to break up. The boundaries were open again.

Britain too had been part of the Roman Empire in the old days. But Saxon invaders had broken in and established kingdoms in England and southern Scotland. By the eighth century they were all, at least nominally, Christians, and the Church had become almost the largest and most powerful owner of riches: in land, cattle, money and objects of gold and silver. This was partly through gifts – some of them no doubt fire insurance against a well-deserved hell – and partly because the Church was a more durable institution in those days than, for instance, a noble or kingly family whose sons were always in hazard of war. Abbots and monks might come and go but the riches of an abbey remained. And remained an obvious target for any raider.

These raiders were the Vikings. At one time they were so successful that they had almost conquered England. At first they only came over in summer after the sowing and before the harvest. There is something very alarming about a swimming snake. It ripples along extra-ordinarily fast with its head staring out in front of it and well up out of the water. These Viking ships were called serpents and their high prows usually had some kind of terrifying head carved and painted on them. The biggest ones of all were called dragons. They were built for speed, especially for a short spurt from the rowers, and might have crews of fifty to a hundred men. But they had to be big enough to take back treasure and perhaps a few captives. At home on the farms they needed slaves – thralls they called them – to do the dirtiest work, though they never really based their economy on slave labour. There were not nearly enough prisoners for that and if a thrall was ever allowed as a rower in one of the boats, he immediately became a free man.

The story of the first Vikings to come to England towards the end of the eighth century is this: three of the serpents came in to the Dorset coast where traders were known and welcomed and the port reeve rode down with the idea of collecting his dues. But the strangers killed him and anyone else they could see, took whatever they could lay their hands on and pushed off the boats. This story shows, I think, that there was already plenty of trade across the North Sea; the new situation comes when traders get the notion that there is more profit in being thieves. During the ninth century they were a constant danger.

They sacked the monastery of Lindisfarne and a few years later they had rounded Scotland, come down the west coast and sacked Iona, killing all the monks. It seems likely though, that by this time there had already been some kind of more or less peaceable settlements in the Orkneys by Norse people. These raiders must have been extremely good seamen; I wouldn't like to go through the Pentland Firth with those boiling tides, round Cape Wrath and down through the Minch in a boat with only a few feet of freeboard, even if I had a good engine. West coast weather seldom holds for more than a day or two at a time and it is no joke landing on the islands. Yet, if you like adventures, if killing people and risking being killed yourself doesn't worry you, and if the alternative is a rather boring life of dull work, perhaps as a younger brother always put upon by the others, not able to marry the girl you want, not having songs and stories made about you, then the Viking life must have been wonderful and the lands of the west would seem the home of treasure and delight which a bold man might snatch at and win.

Even apart from treasure, the land must have seemed very fertile and beautiful to these folk from darkly shadowed fjords and mountains where the snow lies cold till April. They would only just have had time to plough and sow after their hard winter before the longboats were ready to sail. In the farthest north – Ohthere's land – they might have snowstorms at midsummer. Then in the west they would find summer well on with green grass and fat cattle, the corn well up, varied and beautiful trees and flowers and a mild climate. Above all, they would have found this in Ireland where there was a civilisation as old and elaborate as that of Rome, though not so stable and with a different kind of outlook. Ireland could be and was attacked from both sides, beginning in the eighth century with the Danes – the 'black foreigners' – who came round by the English Channel. Then in the ninth century the Norsemen, 'the white foreigners' who had found their way down the Minch, joined in. They fought with the kings and queens of Ireland and occasionally with one another. They brought over their wives and households or intermarried with the Irish. For three centuries it was the Norsemen who held Ireland. One of the linguistic results of this is to be found in the works of James Joyce.

In the ninth century the Viking raids began on the mainland of Europe. After the breaking of Charlemagne's empire they sailed and rowed up the Seine to the walls of Paris, the Frankish capital. They must have attacked from all sides, for Paris in those days was all on the island – *Ile de la Cité*. They say that the city was saved from sackings by a mist that rose from the river followed by sickness. But the Vikings had got a footing on the lower reaches of the Seine and they adventured up others of the main rivers of France.

It is said that the Viking chief who sailed up the Seine was Ragnar Lodbrok, but there are so many stories about him that it is hard to know which are true. This is the traditional story of how Ragnar Lodbrok or Hairybreeks got his nickname. There was a certain king of Sweden who went hunting in the woods and brought home some snakes for his daughter to rear, and this she had to do whether she liked it or not. What it doesn't say in the story is why King Herodd had to bring home this doom, but it was probably because he disobeyed the rule of some god or wood spirit who then wished the snakes or laidly worms on him as a punishment. His daughter, Thora, had to provide a whole ox a day for the snakes to eat and they grew and scorched the countryside with their breath. So the king proclaimed that whoever killed the snakes should have his daughter as bride, and many warriors tried to do this, but all were slain by the laidly worms. But Ragnar asked his nurse (who was probably a fairy in some way in touch with the gods who had put the doom of the serpents on to Sweden) for a woollen mantle and breeches. With these he landed in Sweden and there plunged into water which then froze on him and he went on towards the Swedish palace. Here he was duly attacked by the laidly worms, who tried to bite and poison him, and he fought them for a long time armed in his coat of ice, and at last pierced both their hearts with his spear. Then, of course, he married the Princess and lived happily ever after, so far as that part of the story goes.

This may easily have been invented centuries later. Perhaps Ragnar, son of a small king, was one of these wild young men who had to Go West for adventure, though he is also said to have travelled through Russia. One way and another, according to the stories, he had several wives. One of them was the daughter of Sigurd the Volsung, the slayer of Fafnir the biggest dragon (or banker) of the lot, and his wife Brynhild, the Valkyrie, daughter of Odin. Nor were his other wives less noble and romantic, and he had a great brood of sons who followed him in adventure, while their sisters, granddaughters of the Valkyrie and the man who understood the speech of birds, great granddaughters of the god Odin, embroidered a flag with a magic raven, which spread its wings for victory. But there came a day when the raven drooped its wings and Ubbi, the son of Ragnar Lodbrok, was killed and the banner fell into the hands of the west coast English, desperately countering a Viking attack in the dark days when King Alfred was hiding in the marshes of Sedgemoor. And the English took great heart and the next battle was Ethandun where the King broke the power of the Vikings.

It may be, however, that the 'Sons of Ragnar Lodbrok' were really members of a military brotherhood, young fighters who took or were given the name and embroidered the story. In fact this is really the most probable explanation of the whole thing. Ragnar Lodbrok may have been some kind of divine hero (as divine, say, as Herakles) and even his death may be the echo of a sacrificial end: something to hallow and excite his 'sons'.

It is said that Ragnar Lodbrok, still on his adventures as an old man, was shipwrecked in Northumberland and there taken prisoner and thrown into a pit of serpents, 'How the young pigs would squeal if they knew what the old boar suffers,' he said, but he sang as he died, telling over his battles, ready for the Valkyries who would come galloping down shafts of light to take him away to Valhalla. And soon enough the young pigs knew and went out to avenge him. One of his sons was Ivarr the Boneless (he is said to have been born with a bone too few in the leg, but that did not stop him from being the master mind who organised the Viking raids in the ninth century), and Ivarr had his brothers and half-brothers fighting at his side. Meanwhile other bands of Vikings were doing the same thing in Frisia, rowing up the great rivers, the Rhine, the Elbe and the Scheldt, and establishing base camps on the islands, just as they had done at Sheppey (Sheep Island) and along the sandy English coasts. It was Ivarr who defeated the East Anglians at Thetford and killed Edmund their king, either in battle, or by the martyrdom of the stories – stoning him to death with their after-dinner bones, perhaps in memory of their own Old Boar.

Another of Ragnar's sons, Biorn Ironside, went adventuring farther west yet. Perhaps it seemed by then that England, Scotland and Ireland had no more plunder left in them; perhaps it all seemed too tame. He took the Vestrvegr, the west way, out beyond Ushant to the great bay of the Atlantic, his hand on the steering-oar, the bridle* of the strand-steed, wild deer of linden, bounding over billow, the sledge of summer on the plain of glitter.

* These are just a few examples of the lovely 'kennings', the similes which are showered like stars through the sagas.

By the ninth century Spain, under the Moors, was a highly civilised State where scholars discussed astronomy and mathematics and craftsmen made the best swords in the world. But the Vikings managed to pillage the coastal towns and forced their way up the river to Seville. The Emir who ruled Spain built ships to fight them before they landed, and when the next Viking expedition sailed there were sea battles on the same seas where Nelson was to fight the Spanish ships eight hundred years later. But the Viking fleet under Biorn and his friend Hasting sailed on and through the Pillars of Hercules into the Middle Sea. Here they turned south for a raid on North Africa, which was also part of Islamic civilisation; then north again to raid the coast of Spain and France; they took some Moorish prisoners – blue men, they called them – and later took them back to Ireland. They set up their winter quarters in the marshes of the Camargue in the Rhône delta.

Most likely they were still there in the early spring when the marshes are alive and aflutter with millions of northward-going migrant birds. And they had in their wild heads a plan for the next raid which was to be beyond anything that even a Viking had dreamed: it was the sacking of Rome, of the Eternal City herself.

They knew that Rome was south down the coast of Italy, a great and wonderful city, one would see her towers and domes from the coast. How many days' sail? No doubt they asked the local inhabitants and were answered by shrugged shoulders and gesticulating hands and a torrent of Provençal. But they thought they had the idea. They sailed.

For a time they skirted along a rocky and deserted coast. Beyond and inland were mountains higher and vaster than their own mountains; homes doubtless of stranger monsters and trolls. And in time they came to a beautiful blue sun-warmed bay, and beside it, as they had dreamt, the city. They had their plan ready.

It was Hasting's plan. A messenger was sent to the city to say that a Viking leader was dying and wished to be baptised. In answer to this there came a bishop who baptised Hasting on his sham sick-bed. Next day he 'died' and the same bishop was asked to give him burial in consecrated ground.

The coffin, which was followed by Vikings in black cloaks, was carried to the cathedral and there Hasting leapt out of the coffin and his followers threw off their cloaks and drew swords. The city was theirs and was thoroughly plundered, and it was only after that was finished that they found out that it was not Rome at all, but a small city called Luna.

Hasting was rather given to this kind of craft, but in the end he met his match in Alfred's England. I am inclined to think that we underestimate King Alfred, just because of the cakes and all that. He seems to have been able to turn his mind to every kind of problem and to have made a good job of them all. If he had not had to spend so much time and energy trying to drive out or at least hold back the Vikings, he might have been able to establish a settled Saxon civilisation which would have left a considerable aesthetic and literary mark. Even from what is left, we are bound to recognise the excellent sense of design and fine craftsmanship of the Saxons: something outstanding in west Europe. As it was, Alfred and his successors made England, in the sense that it was recognisably the same country for which Harold Godwinsson fought William of Normandy and for which the Battle of Britain was fought against Hitler's Germany.

For two and a half centuries the eastern side of England and, to a somewhat less extent, Scotland, was being raided, colonised and raided again. All this meant a constant pressure of custom, law and ways of life, even when there was some co-existence between raiders and raided, or when settled Danes took sides with English thegns and ceorls to repel an attack. And all the time other Vikings were raiding and landing all along the other North Sea coasts. Some would be thrown back, but more stayed and many of them took wives. Women were not allowed to come from Denmark or Norway on war-ships, and after all, a man must settle down in comfort. Many of the wives were noble women of the invaded country, and the children might be two-tongued.

And so they would settle down more or less, farming the good land along the broad, smiling river valleys of north-west Europe and protecting them against their original owners or from any fresh wave of invaders that might come. But they were always prepared to go back to their old trade.

We have the names and deeds of many other Viking leaders. Some are well known, but some are forgotten and yet have lived in names or places. Who was Hammer? It was a common enough name for a hard hitter. He brought his serpent into a vik, a muddy creek of the Thames where it was still wide and tidal. With the centuries the ending 'Vik' turned into 'smith', and only a few years ago the creek at

Hammersmith, which had begun to stink in its old age, was filled in and became as though it never was.

All newcomers to a country bring something with them which goes to make up for what they destroy, often indeed to outweigh it. One thing the Vikings taught us was ship-building. King Cnut's dragon ship, built in England, is said to have had sixty oars a side. She must have been a beauty.

SHOCK HEAD TO FAIR HAIR

ABOUT the year 860 in Norway 'King Harald took the kingdom after his father when he was ten winters old. He was the biggest of all men, the strongest and fairest to look on, a wise man and very high-minded'.

It was only too clear what kind of difficulties Harald would have to start with. His father, Halfdan the Black, sledging back from a visit when the spring sun had begun to melt the ice of the water of Rand, fell, as the chronicler said, through the roof of the salmon's house and was drowned. He had been not only a well-liked king but also a lucky one – there had been good harvests in his time. He was a Corn King, a harvest man, and everyone wanted a bit of his luck. So finally they cut up his drowned body, claimed, it might be, as sacrifice by the Water Goddess, All-Mother, and shared it out among the various claimants. Everyone buried his joint in a sacred mound and proceeded to make war on King Halfdan's ten-year-old son, Harald, who might be less of a warrior than his father.

It turned out, however, that the young King and his uncle, Guthorm, between them beat the other kings. But even so Harald's kingdom was no bigger than a modern county, and when Gyda, the daughter of another kinglet, whom he was courting, sent word that she would only marry him if he made himself lord of all Norway, he took an oath that he would never cut or comb his hair until he had become just this. He must have been twelve or thirteen years old at this time.

So season after season he pressed on with his conquest, killing everyone who opposed him and laying claim to all ownerless land. He got the name of conqueror and merciless, and some of the kinglets thought it was better to become Harald's men than to fight. For instance, at Naumdale, there were two brothers called Herlaug and Hrollaug, both of whom called themselves king. They had spent three years building themselves a hall of stone with a timber roof. I think it must have been partly hollowed out of a hill and would have been meant to withstand a siege. And when they heard King Harald and his army were coming they must have thought very hard what to do. King Herlaug decided to have plenty of food and drink brought into the hall, then he went into it with eleven men, and the roof was covered up with stones and turf and that seems to have been the end of them.

'But King Hrollaug went on the top of the hill where all the kings were wont to sit and let array a kingly high-seat and sat down therein. Then he let lay pillows on the bench where all the earls were wont to sit and tumbled himself down from the high seat on to an earl's seat and gave himself the name of Earl.' That is to say, Hrollaug publicly went down a step from king to earl. 'After that fared Hrollaug to meet King Harald and give him up all his realms and prayed to become his man and told him what he had done in all things. Then King Harald took a sword and fastened it on his girdle, then hung a shield about his neck and made him an earl and led him to the high seat. Then he gave him the Naumdale folk and made him earl over them.'

Now this shows very clearly that what King Harald was doing was starting a version of feudalism. It was very much the same as the feudal system which we know in this country. This was brought over by the Normans and lasted until the time when people began to find money was more important than land. The Normans, as we shall see, are very closely related to these folk of Harald's, but they did not take their version of feudalism from Norway; they found it in France and it had quite a lot of Roman law and much Roman thought embedded in it. In fact it had grown naturally out of the economic breakdown of the Roman empire. But Harald seems to have made his own version. Some version was probably inevitable as things were working out.

In a feudal system the land belongs to the king or anyone else with the power to enforce the system: for instance, the great counts in

France and Middle Europe, and sometimes the great abbeys. The king or lord (and vestiges of this still remain when we speak in modern Scottish land tenure of the feu superior) has an obligation to give protection to his lieges. This may mean a good deal if it is properly carried out.

Other people hold their land from the lord. They are his men; they owe him allegiance: fundamentally, that is, they pay him a rent in service. The prime service of the liege to his lord is service in war and peace, his own service and that of his men. He also has to feed and entertain his lord whenever he is asked to do so. This may be a heavy burden if the lord comes round with a whole court of men and women, and the better you treat them the longer they stay. The lord holds courts of justice and punishes wrongdoers; this is part of his protection. The king or lord delegates part of the system of justice back to his lieges so that they too can hold courts and have power of life and death over those who are under them. For the lieges in their turn have lieges of their own, holding land from them on a service of some kind: service in the overlord's war, or service of some other sort, including the provision of food. Right at the bottom (except for serfs or thralls) are the men who hold a few acres in land for service in ploughing, harvesting, road making, wood or peat cutting and so on. But so long as people have to be fed, clothed and housed off the land of their own country, it is the people at the bottom who have to do the work. They have to feed themselves and their families, and any surplus goes into the structure of overlordship. If there is no surplus, the families of the food growers starve. This fact, which becomes particularly obvious in periods of slight agricultural knowledge, when there were often years of no surplus, finally forced itself into the minds of all the people at the bottom. You had to be very stupid not to see it, even though Church and State were both doing their utmost to put the thing into other terms, which would induce the poor labourer to accept his lot, and had a number of means of punishing him on earth and in heaven if he rebelled.

Of course, in times of prosperity and with immense goodwill on all sides it might work. As indeed almost any other system might work in similar circumstances. It was not quite such an elaborate structure as this to start with, in Norway or anywhere else. But that is bound to be the pattern of feudalism anywhere. Later on the services would turn into money rents. But for a long time service was more valuable than money and those who benefited from it tried to keep up feudalism.

It went on for many centuries in Europe, getting increasingly com-
plicated, especially when, for instance, a liege held part of his land
from one lord and part from another. And a whole class of 'clerks'
grew up whose job it was to deal with – and sometimes encourage –
these complications. But war service means one thing: the more lieges
and especially the more powerful lieges a lord can get, the bigger his
power and his army will be and the more new lieges he can bring under
him. And so it goes on merrily until he meets another lord who has as
powerful lieges as he has: then there is the kind of full-scale war that
made parts of Europe into hell during the Middle Ages.

The whole thing rests on the idea that every bit of land belongs in
the first instance to one person or one institution. Though we have got
used to this idea after ten centuries or so, it is really rather an odd idea
and was not, for instance, accepted until recently in the Highlands of
Scotland and cannot be accepted except by a settled community. The
idea that all land belongs to someone would seem crazy, for instance,
to a society of hunters or wanderers of any kind. There is a tragic
conflict of ideas about land at this very moment in the minds of two
different societies of people in East Africa.

And a great many people disliked the idea in Norway. Before
Harald's time the land tenure there had been by heads of families on
the land they farmed, Bonders they called themselves. They never
claimed ownership in the woods and wild country, but only on the
land which they were directly using. They met together in a kind of
parliament, the Thing, and some of them naturally took the lead, and
perhaps called themselves king, but the rest had no formal obligation
to them. But, of course, this state of society was not nearly as efficient
as Harald's feudal system. It lead to endless arguments, delay, jealousies
and people backing out, not doing what they said they were going to
do, just because there was no way of forcing them to do it. In fact it
had all the defects of democracy.

But it had some of the advantages too. It made people feel they were
running their own lives. They couldn't suddenly be called up for
service by the feudal lord in some war that didn't interest them, on
pain of losing their lands. They could sit in their own houses and sulk.
Within the laws which they made themselves they could do what they
liked. In fact they were free. And when King Harald began to try to
force them into this new order of his, they felt they were giving up their
freedom. They resented that more than they wanted the king's protection. They certainly did not realise all the evils of feudalism or the

possibility that their son's sons might get crushed down into the very bottom; it is very difficult to see where any new political system is going to lead in another century or so and probably most of us guess wrong. But I think that some of the Norsemen must have felt rather like people feel nowadays if once they have lived democratically and then suddenly find themselves under another kind of rule. Men who felt like that fled from Norway a thousand years ago, just as people fled from Nazi Germany when Hitler came into power.

So in the late ninth century you will find a great scatter of men travelling out from Norway almost all over the known world, just as Germans and Czechs did in 1938. The following chapters will show in more detail what happened to some of them, and how they kept their own ideas of freedom.

As a matter of fact, King Harald was not in the least like Hitler. He was a big, strong, attractive man, generous, a good friend, and always ready to take advice. Many of the men who became his lieges served him with love and in fine companionship and he feasted on meat and wine and mead and he married at least nine wives, including the original Gyda. They were mostly daughters of kings and kinglets who were now his liege-men and he had a number of children, most of whom did well. They were brought up in the halls of their mothers' folk, for naturally enough most of the mothers stayed a good part of the time in their fathers' original kingdoms. But when he married Ragnhild the Mighty, a daughter of Eric, King of Jutland, he had to keep a great court for her and not see anything of the rest of his wives for three years.

The conquest of Norway went on, battle after battle, with burning of homes and blood and hurt. There was sea fighting too. One winter he built a dragon ship, a great ship holding many picked men, his own guard and the bare-serks; these were men who enjoyed fighting so much and got so wild about it that they fought in their shirts alone without the heavy byrnie, the war shirt of linked metal, that most people wore and that hindered movement a little. They may have used drugs to induce this mood, possibly some kind of wild fungus. They were terrifying and dangerous to have against one, but grand to have with one and any king would try to have some of them on his side. The bare-serks were the forerunners of the professional camps of comrades, the men of Jomsburg and Trelleborg. They had the morals and manners of those who are soldiers only, and if there was no fighting to be done, they might be rather awkward to have about. But for

The king and the bare-serk

twelve years or so of Harald's reign there was always plenty of that.

Harald himself always led his own men. We in whose day war is almost altogether unpleasant must remember that in those days it was for many people the thing they liked best. A summer without a battle was like a winter without a game of football. There would be a good deal of practice fighting and doubtless people would fuss endlessly about their gear, about their place in the battle and about tactics. Part of the reward of a good fighter would be that the *skalds* would make up songs about him, but if he did badly the same *skalds* would mock at him publicly in a manner not to be borne.

So, after about twelve years of fighting, Harald, who was still a young man, became sole king of Norway. And he held a great feast at Mere, the Hall of Earl Rognvald his friend and liegeman. Rognvald had been a Bonder, a free-holder, but he had decided to come in with Harald and the new order of things, and Harald gave him peoples and made him earl of more lands than he had held in the old days, and he was nicknamed the Keen-councilled. It was he who cut Harald's hair now that the vow was fulfilled. It must have been a horrible mat and no doubt crawling with lice; Harald's wives must have had plenty to put up with! Before that they had called him Shockhead, but now that his hair was washed and combed and cut perhaps to shoulder length, you could see that it was beautiful. Because of it Rognvald called him Harald Hairfair.

But meanwhile there were many men, the young men especially who could not bear to have a king over them. Some of them moved out north into the Finns' country. There they lived as people in barren highlands are apt to do, by harrying and pillaging their better-off lowland neighbours. But the lowlanders were King Harald's men and Harald protected them and avenged them and there was constant border war going on. Others went farther afield yet to the Orkneys and the Shetlands and Hebrides and beyond as we shall see, to the Faeroes and Iceland, and some who had fled there stayed on as peaceful colonists and of them we shall hear in the next chapter. But others used these far-out islands as bases for attack on King Harald. In fact they were Vikings, but turned against their homeland. And King Harald would sail to one island after another, clearing out the Vikings, giving no mercy to any of them, and he even came down into Scotland and harried there, killing the men of his own blood and any Scots who fought on their side.

Another of the young men who could not bear to live in Norway under feudalism was actually a son of Rognvald the Keen-councilled, the friend of Harald. His name was Rolf and he was too big to ride the Norwegian horses which must have been more like shaggy ponies. So he went on foot and they called him Rolf the Ganger. He was a great Viking and though he had started furth of Norway, he ended up by carrying off goods and cattle in Norway itself. And the king caught him at it. Harald was furious and summoned the Thing, the parliament of the chief men which still went on meeting, but where the king's word and wish was now all-powerful. Here he gave out that Rolf was an outlaw, a wolf's head to be killed by anyone who had a mind. Rolf's mother, Hild, Rognvald's wife, came to Harald and prayed him to take off this doom which would drive her son for ever away, but Harald would not. Hild made a song against Harald and part of it went like this:

> Ill to be wild in council,
> With wolf of Odin's war-board.
> If he fare wild in forest,
> He'll waste thy flock right sorely.

But Rolf the Outlaw went his ways and won him lands from the Franks in the north-west of their country. Here he settled and his lands filled with Norsemen and came to be called Normandy. His great-great-grandson was Robert Long-sword, the father of William the Bastard who defeated Harold Godwinsson at the battle of Hastings in 1066 and made himself King of England.

After the outlawing of Rolf, Harald reigned for many years as King of Norway, and on the whole, there was peace and settled government, and people had time to plough and sow and reap, and build, and feast, and buy and sell, and make songs and tell stories. And King Harald's sons grew up and every one of them in his mother's district was thought of as possible heir to the throne. So there was trouble of many kinds. We know of one other wife whom King Harald took, Snow-fair, the Witch Maiden, daughter of the Finnish wizard, who gave him a cup of honey-mead and took his heart. They were married and had four sons and Snowfair, the beautiful witch, died, but for three years yet she lay on their marriage bed uncorrupted and for three years the king stayed by her, sorrowing.

Later on one of these sons took to sorcery in a big way. But King Harald, his father, did not like this at all. He sent one of his other sons,

Eric Bloodaxe, the son of Ragnhild the Mighty, to kill him and eighty other wizards, his colleagues. Nor was this the only fighting and killing between Harald's sons and their stepbrothers.

Most of the king's daughters, and there were many of them too, and beautiful, were married to the great earls, so that Harald's blood ran in most families in Norway. And indeed it is likely that this is still so, and the Norwegians think of themselves as the bravest and strongest and most stubborn of all the people in Europe to this day.

THE ISLANDS

WHEN the Norsemen came to the Shetlands, the Orkneys and the Hebrides, they found people there who were called Scots; but these Scots were themselves incomers of a mixed race, partly Gaels and speaking some language akin to modern Gaelic, and partly Brythonic, who built brochs, the enormous round towers which were their fortresses and defences. They must have been a fairly prosperous people, who farmed and hunted and fished and had got to the stage of using iron weapons, tools and pots. Parts of their brochs remain, especially in the outer islands, though even here they have been a good deal pulled down by later people for building stone. The broch at Mousa in Shetland, which has not been pulled about so much, because it is on a lonely island, gives one an idea of what they are like. It is the same size and shape as a cooling tower and looks incredibly menacing there on the green isle. Some of these broch towers may have been low forts, but others went up for at least forty feet and were open at the top – that is the only way the light could come in – and within the enormously thick walls there is always the corkscrew stair with lightless cells off it. In the middle of the space between the walls there is a hearthstone and a water cistern in the rock, and probably there used to be a kind of thatched wooden veranda all round inside the walls or perhaps a conical hut. You can only get in through a narrow low passage through a great wall. The brochs are terrifying places, yet if the outer world were full of dangers they might have seemed wonderfully safe and cosy.

But the people who built the brochs were invaders themselves from some other part of Europe, and the ones who came to the islands must have had boats big enough to take themselves and their gear, including, I think, their sheep, cattle and perhaps horses. Before their time there were other people living in the islands who used bronze but not yet iron. And they in their turn may have been incomers. For we know from the remains of their refuge places and from the remains of pottery, tools and weapons that have been found in their rubbish heaps, the kind of people there were in these islands for a long time, 2,000 years or so before the Norsemen came. And we know, for instance, that the now treeless Outer Hebrides had at one time forests growing on them and no doubt an easier climate, more real soil for growing crops and less peat, so that invaders would find these desirable islands to settle in permanently and in which to build up some kind of civilisation.

What is not quite certain is whether, for instance, the broch at Mousa was still used as a fortress when the Vikings landed, whether the local people drove their sheep into it and tried to hold it. Probably not. Probably by then the brochs were deserted by men and only peopled by the same kind of ghosts that seem to people them still. Later on we hear of 'Mousaberg' being used as a temporary fortress by some of the Norsemen during their own quarrels, and twice a pair of noble lovers sheltered in it.

It seems indeed that in Shetland and Orkney at least there were not many of the Gaels, or, at any rate, many who were powerful enough to be mentioned in the sagas. There was probably a scattered population of small farmers who ran away and took to the hills when the Vikings came, as well as some priests and monks. But on the mainland and some of the Hebrides there was a civilisation at least as advanced as theirs. Most of the Gaels were Christians and relatively many of them became monks. If you didn't want to live the ordinary life, which involved a great deal of killing other people and animals, the alternative was the church. But here you could either live in a community with your own farm – and the monks would experiment with new kinds of fruit and vegetables for instance, which they might get from their brother monasteries in the south – and practise such things as writing, painting and medicine. Or else you might, especially if you were likely to have

deep mystic experience, go away alone to some small island and live
on roots and birds' eggs and whatever God gave you, and cut yourself
off from the less significant world of men. Many a small unpeopled
islet is still called Pabbay, the priest's island.

In some places at least the Norsemen must have lived in amity with
the Gaels, drank and hunted with them. There was plenty of hunting
in Scotland, bears and wolves, deer and wild boar and the noble white,
heavy-maned bulls of the Caledonian forest, with their black muzzles,
ears and hoofs. And there were fur-bearing animals too, out of which
you made mantles for the northern winter and rugs and cushions for
bed or high seat: beavers, martens, pole cats, otters and so on – but no
rabbits; not for another four centuries at least was that pest brought
north from Africa or Spain and let loose by the sportsmen. Seals were
hunted both for fur and flesh and above all the seal oil which was good
both for coughs and colds and was burnt in the stone or shell lamps as it
still was early this century in the crusies on many of the outer islands.
And there was much whale hunting, probably carried out by the whole
population as it is today in the Faeroes.

The islands must have looked the same as they do now; the grim
cliffs and the brilliant glint of the green turf on the heights above, the
crying of the birds, the caves and the great rocks and the thundering
waves. But it was familiar enough to the incoming long-boats and they
would coast around the islands to find in the kyles and the sea lochs,
which are still called voes, the kind of place they wanted. Fair Isle,
between the Shetlands and Orkneys, is now an administrative problem
put by a diminishing population, who, all the same, need communications with the mainland, houses and schools and so on; but then
it was an important naval base.

Vikings must have landed occasionally on all the islands round
Scotland from the eighth century onwards. But they did not settle
there much until the time of Harald Hairfair and the men who could
not bear to go on living under his rule. Harald gave the Shetlands and
Orkneys to his friend Rognvald the Keen-councilled, as over-lord, but
Rognvald gave over both lands to his brother Sigurd and the king
made Sigurd an earl. He was a great fighter and joined with Thorstein
the Red, who came out of Ireland, and who was the son of that remarkable woman, Aud the Deep-minded, whom we shall hear about in the
next chapter. They harried down into Scotland as far as Ross.

There is a story of how Earl Sigurd killed a Scots earl called Melbrigda
Toothy. Melbrigda in Gaelic means the servant or follower of Bridget,

but whether this was Saint Bridget or the earlier goddess of the same name is rather doubtful; and he was nicknamed Toothy because he had a tooth that stuck out of his head. There was a hard battle, the more so because Sigurd had tried to cheat the Scots, but in the end he won and cut off the heads of Melbrigda and all his folk. Then the Norsemen fastened the heads of Melbrigda and his men to their horses' cruppers and rode home, singing and boasting of what they had done. 'Then Sigurd wished to spur the horse with his foot and he struck his calf against the tooth which stuck out of Melbrigda's head and scraped it and in that wound there sprung up swelling and that led him to his death.' So that was the end of Earl Sigurd.

After that one of Rognvald's sons took up the earldom, but he did not protect his own men from some Danish Vikings who came on a landing party. That meant he had failed in his duty as a feudal over-lord; so he gave up his earldom and went back to Norway. Everyone thought very badly of that. Then Einar, the youngest of Rognvald's sons, tall, ugly and one-eyed, offered to go out. His father gave him a ship of twenty benches, that is to say, forty rowers, and perhaps as many more men of a crew. He had a battle in Orkney with the Danish Vikings and killed them. He was the first of the Norsemen to take to burning peats – there was plenty of wood at home in Norway – so that they nicknamed him Turf Einar. Einar's next enemy was Halfdan Longleg, one of the sons of King Harald and Snowfair the witch. Halfdan and his brother had killed Earl Rognvald, so according to the morals of the time, Einar was within his rights to offer up Halfdan as a blood sacrifice to Odin, by cutting his ribs away from his backbone and pulling his lungs out in the traditional manner of the 'blood eagle', and in the end appeasement was made between him and King Harald. After that the Orkneys and Shetland were ruled by a succession of Norse earls, most of whom met bloody deaths. From time to time the kings of Norway attempted to assert a real suzerainty over them and imposed Christianity of a kind. King Olaf Trygvasson, for instance, seized on the little son of the reigning Earl and threatened to kill him then and there if his father would not 'listen to my preaching of the blessed message'. The king continued, 'I shall kill your son before your eyes this instant unless you and your men will serve my God.' People tend to get very passionate about their ideologies.

Still there was a considerable hangover from the old days, and spae-men, who practised sorcery and were probably the remains of the old priests, had a good deal of influence. They foretold the future. And

3*

occasionally there would be outbreaks of sacrificing. The older men would have felt uncomfortable without such familiar things; they would have been afraid the crops would fail.

And so, for centuries, the northern islands and usually part of the mainland were under Norse rule and both place names and people's names there are still mostly the Norse names only half-Scotified. For instance, the name Ganson is really Gunnarsson. For that matter many Highland names go back to the Norsemen; Macaulay is really MacOlaf – son of Olaf. MacDougal means son of black foreigners – the Danes. And the Hebridean Christian name Norman is Tormad (or Thormad) but that again might come from the Irish form Diarmid. Perhaps, though, the names are not really related but, because they sounded alike, they were easily interchanged. There is a look and temper of Norse folk about the Shetlanders and Orkneymen to this day and an abrupt manner of speech, very different from the verbal embroideries of the Gael. When a boat comes into Lerwick, the county town of Shetland, from Norway, it is still 'our people', but if it is a Wick drifter it is 'from Scotland' – another country.

They settled and built their halls along the coast of Caithness and down to Easter Ross and along the north coast of Sutherland: the high cliffs where the tiny thorny rose bushes grow and from which, on a summer day, you see the Orkneys glittering like silver across the sea. Even small islands like Stroma had halls built on them and were ship bases; they were more important at that time than they are ever likely to be again. Some of the Norse men were for ever warring in the Hebrides, but it does not seem as though they had ever settled there for very long. On the other hand, when they *did* settle peaceably we know very little about it, because living in peace does not make 'history'. The saga-writers liked to have battles to describe. They tell of the Vikings who went farther south, down to the Isle of Man, and from there in turn they harried the coasts of Wales and sailed down even to the Scillies and perhaps into the Helford River, the nearest thing Cornwall has to a fjord. Wherever they went there are the place names still, and the government of the Isle of Man is based on Norse forms.

King Magnus Barelegs (so-called because he wore a kilt) in the eleventh century was one of the farthest farers; he was a great warrior and sailor and himself one of the best bowmen of his time. But something very odd happened in one of his sea-battles. A young man also called Magnus, the son of the Earl Erlend of Orkney, whom he had with him as a hostage, and who had been as keen on fighting as the next lad, suddenly refused to put on his armour or take up his spear or sword. He sat down in the middle of the ship, in the middle of the sea-battle; he said he had nothing against anyone there and he would not fight. Then he sang psalms out of his psalter and did not shelter himself. This was the sign of conversion of Magnus of Orkney, who later became first an earl and then a saint.

It was in the course of King Magnus Bareleg's war with Malcolm, King of Scots, that he got Kintyre by craft. Malcolm had promised him all the western lands between which and the mainland he could sail with a fixed rudder. 'But when King Magnus ran in from the south to Kintyre, he made them drag a cutter over the neck of Kintyre, but he held the tiller, and so took as his own all of Kintyre. That is better than the best isle in the southern isles save Man. It goes from the west of Scotland and has a narrow neck of land at the top of it, so that there ships are very often drawn over.'

It is clear from this that the ships, in spite of their length, must have been built more lightly than a modern boat of the same size. And the Vikings must have thought it worth all the labour of hauling, pre-sumably on wooden rollers up the hill from the West Loch and down into Loch Tarbert – half a mile of hauling – rather than sail round the Mull of Kintyre. But these are dangerous waters. Many a good ship has been lost off the Mull, and the modern fishing-boats would always rather go the slow way round, by the Crinan Canal, instead of round-ing Kintyre. And these Norse boats could only sail with the wind abaft the beam; it would be queer weather that would take you due south and then due north. And rowing would be no more use in these tides than a very small auxiliary engine.

The boy, Magnus, who saw the pointlessness of fighting for its own sake – and that was a considerable moral jump to have made – seems to have been an excellent ruler, just and gentle and wise, not afraid of the rich and generous to the poor, besides fighting well when there was real need for it. But his cousin, the other earl, Hakon, grew increasingly jealous of him and surprised him with an army of fol-lowers, in Easter week of the year 1115. Earl Magnus went to meet him, refusing to let his own men defend him. He offered to go on a pilgrim-age to Rome or to remain in prison, but Earl Hakon would accept nothing but his death. Magnus fell on his knees to pray and Hakon ordered first one and then another of his men to kill the good earl. It fell to Lifolf, the cook, who wept aloud and was comforted by Earl

Magnus, who forgave him and all his enemies, but said, 'Hew me a mighty stroke on the head, for it is not fitting that high-born lords should be put to death like thieves.' So this high-born lord and saint died, and very soon miracles began to show at his burial place, so that pilgrims came to Birsay in the Orkneys, mostly from the Shetlands, and were cured of their ills, including leprosy, blindness, and quite a lot of mixed madness. So it became plain that Magnus was truly a saint, and later on a cathedral was built to house his relics. And a few years after the murder, Earl Hakon went on a pilgrimage to Rome and then to Jerusalem. He bathed in the river Jordan and brought away relics, and when he came back he became a good and peaceable ruler and law-giver, and the Orkney men thought he was the best earl they had yet had.

The 16th of April remained as the feast day of Saint Magnus the martyr. There are hymns and his life-story told in prose readings with verse responses in which *Felix Orcadia* rhymes with *exultat curia*. The whole story was put into dog-Latin with love and care:

> *Haco Magni terras et praedia*
> *Sibi subdens invasit omnia,*
> *Contra mitem furit insania.*

There was another Mass for the Translation of Saint Magnus on the 16th of December. Here again the story is told, including the healings and the bringing safe home of ships, but not the story of the gamester who had staked and lost his boat and in desperation called on Saint Magnus who got him two sixes and an ace. The verses go to a great swing:

> *Quos nos esse te laudantes,*
> *Tuum festum celebrantes*
> *Perpetuo Magne tuo*
> *Impetres colloquio:*
> *Ut erepti tua prece*
> *Nos ab hostis saevi nece*
> *Collaetemur, et privemur*
> *Gehennae supplicio.*   Amen.

THE LAND THE RAVENS FOUND

THE first travellers who are known to have reached Iceland were
the Irish monks some time in the seventh century, though it seems
likely that there were actually a few inhabitants some hundreds of
years earlier. It may be that our own folk from Scotland went farther
and more daringly in their skin coracles or curraghs than we can con-
ceive of now. People who have actually worked with a curragh, including Dr Lethbridge, say that they are remarkably seaworthy, as well
as speedy, once one gets the hang of them. We do know for certain
that the monks had already found their way to the Faeroes and indeed
there was probably a small Celtic population there already, living on
fish and mutton and the sea-birds that are still eaten in the Faeroes, and
perhaps cultivating the same small fields that are still cultivated. Why
did they go on north-west into the edges of the Frozen Sea? They may
have heard vaguely of another land, they may have thought that it
was their duty to bring Christianity to it. They may have thought
there were short cuts to paradise. They may have been certain of
oppression if they stayed. Or they may have wanted to go to some far
and lonely place to meditate undisturbed on God. The Irish monk,
Dicuil, who wrote his book early in the ninth century, tells us about
certain priests who had been on Iceland from February 1st to August

1st. They told that 'not only at the time of the summer solstice, but also during the days before and after, the setting sun at evening conceals itself as it were behind a little mound, so that it does not grow dark even for the shortest space of time, but whatsoever work a man will do, even picking lice out of his shirt, he may do it just as though the sun were there'.

Probably there never was a very big Irish population in Iceland, even including the priests. But it is quite certain that they were there when the first Norsemen came. It is said that the priests sailed away from the heathen invaders back to Ireland. Some of the Irish would have been kept as thralls or allowed to stay on in their poor huts, though the Norsemen would surely have taken any decent land. But between these original settlers and the Celtic slaves brought in by the Norse settlers, the Icelanders became less Norse than we would think from their names. The present blood groups in Iceland are very like those in Ireland or western Scotland.

It seems as if the Norsemen found Iceland rather accidentally, though no doubt they had heard rumours of it. But it is said of one that when in the Pentland Firth 'a gale broke his moorings and he was driven west into the sea' and of another that he was a Viking outlawed everywhere, except in the Faeroes where he had his base, and he too was blown west by a gale. Both men praised the new island and called it Snowland.

But the next man definitely meant to get to Snowland; he was a real explorer and his name was Floki Vilgerdsson. He lived in the second half of the ninth century. 'He made ready a great sacrifice and hallowed three ravens which were to tell him his way. They built a cairn when the sacrifice had been made and they called it Floki's cairn.' The raven was Odin's bird of council and no doubt the sacrifice was to Odin. Probably the ravens were sprinkled with the blood of the sacrifice.

'He sailed out to sea with the three ravens which he had hallowed in Norway. But where and when he let loose the first, he flew back to the bows; the second flew up in the air and back to the ship; the third flew north from the bows to the quarter where they found land. They made it on the east at Horn. Then they sailed along the south of the land. But when they sailed west round Reekness and the firth began to open, so that they could see Snowfellness, Faxe' – he must have been one of Floki's crew – 'said, "This must be a big country which we have found; here are great rivers." It was afterwards called Faxe's mouth or bay. Floki and his men sailed west along the Broad firth and then went in towards the land in a firth called Waters-firth or River-firth, over against Bard-strand. The whole firth was full of fish, seals and whales, and for the sake of the fishing they took no heed to make hay, and all their livestock died in the winter. It was then very cold. Then Floki walked northward to a mountain whence he could see a firth full of sea-ice, wherefore they called the land Iceland.'

This means that there was no floating ice to the south of Iceland. In general there is little reference to ice round Iceland or seen on the voyages, until much later. Perhaps at this time the polar icecap was not permanent. At any rate the weather seems to have been more favourable to mankind for several centuries.

Floki's story shows how old is the name Faxo Bay – the place from which so much of our trawled cod comes. Floki stayed a year and when he came back he spoke ill of the new country. But two of his men spoke better of it and one of them said that 'butter dripped out of every blade of grass'. So, of course, he was nicknamed Butter; just as he would have been in any fishing village today.

All this is told in the beginning of the Landnáma Bóc, the chronicles of the beginning of Iceland. This book is largely a collection of notes about the early settlers and their families. Half the men and some of the women had nicknames like Squint or Far-Sailer or The Yeller or Goblin-crusher or The Fool. The book is made up of quantities of rather disjointed paragraphs and many of them are like the bones of a short story. Here, for instance, is one showing, very typically, the relation between the people and the place names: 'Ketil-Beorn was the name of a nobleman in Nean-dale. He was the son of Ketil and Asa, the daughter of earl Hacon, Grit-Garth's son. He had to wife Helga daughter of Thord Beardie. Ketil-Beorn came to Iceland when the land was broadly settled along the sea. He had the ship that is called *Ellide*. He put into the mouth of Ellide's river, north of Blue-shaw-heath. He stayed the first winter with Thord Beardie, his father-in-law.

'But in the spring he went up over the Heath to seek him a good choice of land. They had a sleeping-place there, and he built them a hall at the place that is now called Hall-brink in Blue-Shaw. But when they went hence they came to a river, which they called Axe-water, because they lost their axe there. They took up their abode for a while under the mull of the hill, which they called Trout-mull, for there they left behind (forgetting them) the river-trout they took out of the river.

'Ketil-Beorn took in settlement all Grim's-ness up from Hauscoll's beck, and all Bath-dale and all Bishops Tongue up to Stack's-water and he dwelt at Moss-fell.

'Ketil-Beorn was so rich in money that he bade his sons cast a cross-beam of silver for the temple that they were about building, and they would not. Then he drove the silver up on the fell behind two oxen, and Hake his thrall, and Bot his bond-woman. They buried the treasure there so that it has never been found since. He killed Hake at Hake-pass and Bot at Bot-pass.'

The story is magnificently clear. If his sons (he had ten children) refused to let him give away the family silver to the temple, for the sake of the fame it would bring him, he was going to see that they would never have it. He had to take someone to help him haul and bury the silver, but he made very certain that they should not be able to give the secret away. Thus, although only thralls, their names were kept in remembrance. Perhaps, indeed, that was promised them before their death. On the other hand it is possible that the later chronicles had decided that if they did not know about a place name, they would at least invent a good story for it.

Most of the first settlers in Iceland were from Norway or south Sweden, and some came from the Hebrides or the north of Scotland. Here is a story of Aud, the Deep-minded (or Deeply-Wealthy). She was the widow of a Viking, Anlaf the White, who had made himself king of Dublin. Aud's son Thorstein was killed in battle and she made up her mind to leave Scotland and find herself a home in a new land. She had a ship built secretly in the forest of Sutherland (there are no trees near the Sutherland coast today) and carried down to the sea; then she sailed. She herself was in command of the expedition, but with her was her granddaughter Thorgerd, whose husband Coll was a man whom Aud held in great esteem, and she had twenty freed men – men who had been her thralls or slaves.

'Yrp was the name of a freeman of Aud's. He was the son of earl Maelduin of Scotland, who fell before Earl Sigurd the Mighty*. The Mother of Yrp was Muirgheal daughter of Gelomael, king of the Irish. Earl Sigurd took them as booty and made slaves of them. Muirgheal was bondmaid to the earl's wife and served her faithfully. She was cunning in many things. She took care of Earl Sigurd's Lady-wife's child while she was in bonds. Afterwards Aud bought her at a high price, and promised her her freedom if she would serve Thorrid

* The same man who killed (and was killed by) Melbrigda Toothy.

the wife of Thorstein the Red, as she had served her lady. Muirgheal and Yrp her son went to Iceland with Aud.'

In spite of the fact that by this time the Icelandic coast must have been fairly well known, Aud had a difficult landing in Iceland, for the boat came ashore at 'Pumice-links† and was wrecked there. She went to Keel-ness to Helgi Beolan, her brother. He asked her to stay with him, and half her company with her; but she thought that was a mean offer, and said that he was a poor-spirited fellow as he had always been. She then went west to Broad-firth to her brother Beorn. He came to meet her with his house-carles; for he said he knew his sister's proud heart and he asked her to his house with all her men; and she accepted this offer.

'Afterwards in the spring, Aud and her company went into Broad-Firth to explore the land. They took their day meal at a place north of Broad-firth, which is now called Day-meal-ness. Afterwards they went inland through the island channels, and landed at the ness, where Aud lost her comb, and this ness she called Comb-ness.

'Aud took in settlement all the Dale-lands, at the inward of the firths, from Day-meal-ness to Scram-leap-water. She dwelt at Hwam, on the Trout-water bay at a place called Aud's-tofts. She had her prayer-place at Cross-hillocks. There she had crosses set up, for she was baptised of the true faith. Her kinsmen afterwards used to hold these hillocks holy, and a barrow or high-place was made there and sacrifice offered.'

Aud gave land to her shipmates and freedmen, so that each of them could set up on his own and farm.

'Cetil was the name of a man to whom she gave land from Scram-leap-water to Haurd-dale-water. He dwelt at Cetil-stead. He was the father of Westlide and of Einar, the father of Clamp-iron and of Thorbeorn, whom Styr slew, and of Thordis the mother of Thorgest.

'Haurd was the name of a shipmate of Aud. To him she gave Haurd-dale. Vifil‡ was the name of a freedman of Aud's. He asked why she did not give him a homestead as she had to the others. But she said it did not matter, because everybody would know he was a gentleman wherever he was. She gave him Vifil's-dale. There he dwelt and had a feud with Haurd. The son of Vifil was Thorbeorn, the father of Gudrid,

† Or lava-links. The lava from the volcanoes comes right down to the sea in some places.

‡ This might come from some Gaelic word like *fiachail*, meaning respectable or important.

whom Thorstein, the son of Erik the Red, had to wife, and afterwards
Thorfin Karlsefne. From him are the bishops come – Beorn, Thorlac
and Brand.'

Very likely Vifil was the son of a Scots or Irish chief, whom Anlaf
the White had captured. We shall hear again of his granddaughter
Gudrid and her husband, Thorfin Karlsefne. In the days of the Greeks,
if a man was captured and made a slave he felt that, as Homer said,
'his manhood was taken away from him'. But Aud could say to the
man who had been her slave that he was a gentleman, and he would
feel like one and be treated as one by everyone else.

'Hound* was the name of a freedman of Aud's, a Scottish man. To
him she gave Hound-dale and there he dwelt a long while.

'Sunk-Wolf was the name of a freedman of Aud's. To him she gave
Sunk-wolf-dale. He dwelt at Broad-bowster and many a man is come
from him.

'To Yrp, the son of Earl Maelduin who was spoken of above, Aud
gave his freedom and Sheep-fells-land. From him the Erplings are
come.'

This shows the way in which Iceland was settled and how people of
mixed countries worked in together and after a few generations all
became one people. Aud herself lived to be an old woman 'so that she
did not rise before noon, and she went early to bed. She let no-one
bother her with any business from the time she went to bed in the
evening until she was dressed, and she answered sharply if anyone
asked her how she was.' She decided that her favourite grandson,
Anlaf, was to inherit her land and she wanted him to get married. He
agreed and she said she would like to have the marriage feast at the
end of summer, because that was the time when it was easiest to get
plenty of food for all their friends who were sure to come. She added
that this was the last feast she meant to give. Anlaf, who was very fond
of his grandmother, said yes, but that he was not going to let his wife
take the rule of the household out of her hands.

All the family came, including her two brothers, and many of her
old ship-mates, and all the big farmers and landowners from the west
settlement of Iceland, probably hundreds of men and women, for they
would all bring some of their own friends and men-at-arms and servants.
Aud would surely have arranged tents or light huts for them to sleep
in. Aud slept late but yet 'she was afoot when the guests came and
went to meet them and welcomed her kinsmen and friends with

* Cu as in Cu-chullan.

courtesy. And when the hall was all set men were mightily taken with the splendour of this feast.'

After that she made a solemn declaration that her lands and wealth were to go to her grandson Anlaf and spoke to everyone and saw that all the guests had what they needed, 'and when she walked briskly out down the hall, men broke into speech saying she was indeed a princely lady'. They drank through the evening until it was bed-time, and the next morning Anlaf went to the bed-chamber of Aud, his grand-mother, and when he came into the room, there was Aud sitting up in the bed, but she was dead. Anlaf went out into the hall and told them what had happened, and everyone was greatly impressed at the way that Aud had kept up her noble bearing until her death-day itself. So now Anlaf's bridal and Aud's wake were both drunk together, and on the last day of the feast Aud was carried to the barrow that was pre-pared for her. She was laid in a ship in the barrow, and much riches laid in with her, and the barrow was closed over her.'

But it also says in the Landnáma Bóc – and nobody can tell which version is right – that when she died she was buried on the shore, below high-water mark, as she had ordered it herself, for she did not wish to lie in unhallowed ground seeing she was a baptised woman. 'But after this the faith of her kinsfolk went wrong.' What this means is that there was no church anywhere near where she could have been buried in consecrated ground, so that she was buried below high-water mark which came to the same thing as being buried at sea. And after that the family became heathen again.

The Icelanders were not on the whole Christians even in name until the time of Olaf Trigvasson in the second half of the tenth century and even then they went on doing some very odd things, especially when they were in difficulties. But the men who wrote the Landnáma Bóc in the twelfth or thirteenth century were all Christians, probably monks, so naturally they put their own emphasis and interpretation on to the doings of their forebears and, doubtless, felt it only right to tell unpleasant stories about the ancestors of those who were behaving badly in the present. Also, of course, they wrote a great deal about their first bishops, most of whom had very adventurous lives, usually including a shipwreck or two. Here is one other settler from the Hebrides who was a first cousin of Aud.

'Aurlyg was the name of a son of Hrapp, the son of Beorn Buna. He was a foster-son of Bishop Patric, the saint in the Southreys. A yearn-ing came upon him to go to Iceland, and he prayed Bishop Patric that he would give him an outfit. The bishop gave him timber for a church and asked him to take it with him, and a plenarium and an iron church bell and a gold penny and consecrated earth to lay under the corner posts.' The church was dedicated to Columcille (Saint Columba of the Cells).

'Then spake Bishop Patric: "Wherever thou turnest in to land, dwell only there where three fells can be seen from the sea and a firth running between each fell, and a dale in each fell. Thou shalt sail to the southernmost; there shall be a shaw there, and further south under the fell thou shalt light on a clearing and three stones set up there. Do thou raise thy church and homestead there."

'Aurlyg put to sea and in a second ship with him a man named Coll, his sworn brother. They kept company out. On board Aurlyg's ship was a man whose name was Thorbeorn Sparrow; another called Thorbeorn Talcni; the third Thorbeorn Scuma. They were the sons of Beadwere Bladder-head. But when they came where they might look out for land, there arose a great storm against them and drove them west about Iceland. Then Aurlyg called upon Bishop Patric, his foster-father, to bring them ashore and vowed that he would give the place a name after his name wherever he should first come ashore. And after that they were but a little while ere they got to land; and he brought his ship to Aurlyg's haven and called the firth Patric's firth therefore. But as for Coll he called upon Thor. They were parted in the storm, and he reached the place called Collswick and there his ship was wrecked. His crew got to land some of them.

'And in the spring Aurlyg fitted out his ship and sailed away with all that he had; and when he came south* of Faxe's bay, he saw the fells that had been spoken of to him, and knew them. And then the iron bell fell overboard and sunk in the sea. But they sailed in along the firth, and went into land at the place that is now called Sand-wick or Keel-ness and there lay the iron bell in the sea-weed.

'Aurlyg took up his abode at Clay-rock by the advice of Helge Beolan his kinsman, and took land in settlement between Mogils river and Oswif's becks. He built a church at Clay-rock as was commanded him.' Which only shows one should always do what the bishop says: at least, I am sure that is the moral which Are, Thorgil's son, who wrote it all down, would like us to learn from it!

All the early settlements were around the coast wherever there was space for a homestead. Many of the ships with their crews of settlers

* North fits the map better.

must have sailed far enough, nosing into one creek or bay after another. There were quarrels over land, for the population grew very quickly and the centre of Iceland, which is all glaciers and icy mountains and volcanoes, is uninhabitable. Probably some people, even in those early days, used the hot springs for bathing and cooking, though not as is done now, for heating greenhouses, growing carnations and even bananas.

These explorers and settlers felt they must assert themselves as true Norsemen. They still lived in the same kind of halls, subject to the fact that most wood had to be imported; they farmed as far as possible as they did in Norway and stuck to the old democratic way of life among equal landholders, who met at the Thing for justice and law-making. One of their very first concerns was to establish their own laws and customs, partly designed to stop anyone from becoming an over-lord or king, or setting up the kind of feudal system which they and their fathers hated and had fled from. The Icelanders kept up the old forms of government very carefully, and the forms of procedure were learnt by heart and written down early on. In fact they became rather too stratified, so that it was difficult to alter them when other things changed. But one can see why they did it. In practice the system worked out as a balance of power between districts and landholders; a major decision of the Thing could only be enforced if you had power on the winning side. If you had not, the decision was unrealistic and probably some excuse was found to alter it. A lot of the sagas turn on legal decisions, the discussions before they were made and how they were enforced or not enforced. But if you were sufficiently determined you could usually shift things around, whether you were man or woman, rich or poor, and a kind of rough justice does come out of it all.

A boy or girl would be brought up in an atmosphere of sayings, some profound, others merely canny. Some warn against common failings, especially 'the heron of forgetfulness which hovers over ale drinking'. The individual quality most valued is common sense – but it should be expressed. The good man is a good counsellor, witty, a social being. He should travel but not stay too long in one place: 'a friend becomes a nuisance if he stays too long in someone else's house.' He should stick up for himself and not be ashamed even if he is poor. He should not quarrel with a fool: 'generally, when a worse man starts quarrelling, the better man retires.' Sayings, like these from the Hávamál, and many others, would be in people's mouths, much as the sayings of Homer were in the mouths of the Greeks, or as people in this country

The ancient domination

quoted the Bible until recently. They were brought over from the old country, along with everything else.

For the settlers must have brought almost everything, to begin with. They brought sheep, cattle, horses, probably poultry and pigs and goats. If they wanted to make a home, they would have to bring some timber at least. And they would have taken weapons, cooking-pots, cups and dishes, farm implements and tools, looms and spinning-gear, shears and needles and so on – a woman might have a box of valuable embroidery threads, gold and silver among them – and also a few chests, beds, tapestries or hangings, an occasional jewel, and perhaps pieces for indoor games which would be needed in the winter nights that were even longer than those in Norway.

They would bring seed corn too, oats and barley and perhaps rye, which would have succeeded well enough in most years, during the climatic conditions round about A D 1000. There might be kale, possibly some herbs, including garlic, though not our type of garlic, which would not do well so far north, but much of the food would be meat, fresh in summer and salt in winter: fish, fresh, smoked, dried and salted, and various preparations of milk. Most of the butter was probably salted. They made their own beer and mead and sometimes cranberry or crowberry wine. They would have imported honey. I doubt if bees could ever do well in Iceland. They seem to have had two solid meals a day, one fairly early in the morning, the other at the end of the day, no doubt lasting until late.

In famine times they ate horse, but Christians were supposed not to, as it was the usual sacrificial animal, in the Teutonic countries anyhow. You could do a lot of magic with horse's heads, too, even before Cocteau. We ourselves and other descendants of horse sacrificers have the remains of an irrational, uncomfortable feeling about horse-meat, which is really no worse than a lot of beef.

Each homestead would have its bath-house. Ordinarily you took your steam bath lying on a bench in the bath-house, where water was poured over hot stones and the steam swirled up and the bather sweated and coughed but felt wonderfully clean at the end of it. Many of the settlers must have been delighted with the Icelandic hot springs all ready made for their bath-houses.

Ten years or so after the first explorers came, Iceland was a settled country full of homes. In fact you get a curious feeling of respectability about it, for the first time in history since, perhaps, the Roman republic. This may be due partly to the fact that there were no obvious external enemies, so the pattern of offensiveness – the warrior always ready to spring on his enemies – did not have to develop. Nature was something of an enemy, but it is a respectable thing to fight nature, whether as farmer or fisherman, engineer, doctor or scientist. There was an element of all of them in the Icelanders. The next set of men to travel the Swan's Road were those who did not fit into this respectable pattern.

It seems doubtful whether there was much visual art, other than carving, whether in wood or walrus ivory. That was something which could be done by hand feel, in the winter evenings. Poetry was the art most practised. Every district would have its poet, who would be particularly skilled, as indeed poets should be, in making topical poems, some very witty. There was much buying and selling and visiting and feasting for betrothals or any family occasions; and for every occasion you would have a poem. The Icelanders were as fond of going to law as the Scots were a thousand years later; part of their pleasure in meetings of the Thing was to be involved in a lot of lawsuits, or to be asked by one's friends for a legal opinion: which might even be as well thought out and praiseworthy as a poem.

The coming of Christianity did not stop any of these things. A few people seemed to have found it upsetting, but most took it calmly enough. It did stop a certain amount of cruelty and gave those who were naturally decent and kindly a good social reason for their conduct. It may, for instance, have induced them not to kill any remaining Christian Celts; but that is only a guess. Probably a good many of them were killed, but people felt rather ashamed of it, invented some excuse or at least never let it get into history.

Christian ethics were nothing startlingly new. They had heard already: 'Show kindness to the poor.' 'Never rejoice in evil.' 'Conduct yourselves blamelessly towards your kinsfolk. You ought not to take vengeance though they give you cause. It is said that this will benefit a man after death.' Christianity stretched all this farther, took away some of the fears of sorcery and the Unknown, or gave a new kind of protection. But it never came with the apocalyptic content that it has always had when it has been taken as their religion by slaves or those in conditions of similar mass oppression. The Icelanders never thought of the Crucified as someone who had died a slave's death and could be identified with the sufferings and hopes of slaves. Odin, Allfather, the Wanderer, had in one of his manifestations, hung nine nights on a tree in the freezing north, wounded with a spear, 'given to Odin, myself to myself'. It was the same pattern of God-head.

Nor did Christianity become much involved, here, with power politics and passions. In fact it tended to be a domestic rule of conduct, a quiet ordering of human ways and a practical fellowship. And it provided shelter and a reason of life for those who were interested in learning and might otherwise have never found a like-minded group.

But some groups were little affected by it, especially those whose conditions were such that they did not find kindliness and neighbourly conduct attractive or indeed possible. It is on the whole amongst them that a new wave of restlessness started, bringing a longing for the Swan's Road, with its own ethics built out of its own necessities, and its own promised land at the far side. And so, here and there they set sail, heading into the same west which had drawn them before.

AUD'S BLOOD

ON the way out to Iceland, Aud the Deep-minded had stopped at the Faeroes, the sheep islands, a good half-way house; doubtless they took in food, refilled the water-casks and did any running repairs that were needed. And Aud arranged a marriage for her grand-daughter Olof, another daughter of Thorstein the Red. Their descendants became the chief family in the Faeroes, the Goteskeggs. And the years went by and now it was the time when Harald Greycloak, grandson of Harald Hairfair, was reigning in Norway and Blue-tooth Harald in Denmark. The King of Norway claimed over-lordship of the Faeroes, but it was a far cry. Still, there was much coming and going across the seas and whatever happened in one place would be heard about sooner or later in the other, whether or not the tribute money arrived in good time.

Quarrels were bad enough in Iceland, but the Faeroes were smaller and it was harder to get away from a feud once it started. There was one such quarrel and most of those in it were descendants of Aud, cousins. Things got worse and worse, with insults and wounding and at last two of the one side were caught on an outlying island with their young sons, a nine-year-old and an eleven-year-old. Both the fathers were killed, but the other side in the quarrel could not find it in their hearts to kill the boys. 'That summer a ship came from Norway to the Faeroes. Hrafn was the name of the steersman . . . he often sailed to Holmgard . . . the ship came in at Thorshaven.'

Now the great-uncle of the boys, who had been one of the party that had killed their fathers, and had taken them away, saying he would bring them up, came to Hrafn, saying he had two slave boys to sell: 'two boys in white-hooded cloaks and short-cut hair; fair featured but with faces swollen with tears.' Hrafn understood who they were and refused to buy them, but Thrand, the great-uncle, gave him money instead, bargaining that the boys should be taken away overseas. And that was how it was, but the next year, when Hrafn had taken them across to Norway and looked after them well, he gave them the money and told them to go seek their fortunes. Sigmund and Thorir were now ten and twelve. Meanwhile Thrand ruled the whole of the Faeroes 'and no-one dared say anything against him'.

Two years went by and the two boys had spent all their money and decided to go east, so they set off across the Dovrefell, no doubt meeting the Great Boyg and other terrors, got lost, lay out in the snow and at last dragged themselves, wet and cold and starving, into a little valley, where an outlaw had set up house. The women of the house looked after them till the outlaw came back 'dressed in reindeer skin with a reindeer on his back'. At first he was angry, but he could not help liking the boys, especially the younger, Sigmund, who at fifteen killed the great, grim wolf-grey wood bear. The outlaw with his wife and daughter had lived alone for many years on the edge of the wild mountains, and his daughter Thurid fell in love with young Sigmund, and before Sigmund left they had plighted troth.

For Sigmund knew he would never get vengeance for his father unless he took service with some over-lord and made a name for himself. So he went to Earl Hakon of Norway who had succeeded King Harald Greycloak. The earl had known his father, so he got friendship and protection and the chance of proving himself as raider and warrior. He and his cousin and devoted friend Thorir went off raiding, first from other Viking ships, then from the Steward and other great men who were under the King of Sweden. All this was very pleasing to Earl Hakon, who next sent him out to the Orkneys to deal with an old enemy of his called Harold Ironhead. This went less well for Earl Hakon, because Sigmund and Harold Ironhead each thought the other was a man after his own heart, and they made peace with one another. At first Earl Hakon would not have it, but when young Sigmund threatened to leave him, he too reluctantly swore peace with his old enemy.

And now Sigmund told the earl that he and Thorir wanted to finish with this plundering and go out to the Faeroes for their revenge and good name. Hakon said it was no use trying to land on the surf-beaten rocks of the Faeroes in a long-ship, the ordinary ship of war, but he would have two merchant ships built for him, which would be more seaworthy. So the ships were built and when all was ready Earl Hakon asked Sigmund in what he put his trust. 'In my strength and good right arm,' said Sigmund.

But the earl said he would do better to put his trust in Thorgerda Holgabrud. So they went to a wood and along a little path in the wood, and there in a clearing was a house with a wooden fence. And whether it was the house of a witch or a goddess, it was wonderfully beautiful with carving on it all covered with gold and silver. Within there were many gods and many windows and on the end bench Thorgerda Holgabrud, most splendidly dressed.

'The earl cast himself down before her feet and lay there long, and then he stood up and said to Sigmund that they should make her some offering, and put silver on the stool before her. "And we will notice how she will take it," said the earl, "for I wish she shall let go the ring she has on her arm. And you, Sigmund, will get help from the ring if you have it."' So at last the earl got the arm-ring from Thorgerda Holgabrud and gave it to Sigmund and made him promise that he would never part from it. That ring is part of the story.

So Sigmund sailed back to the Faeroes with his friend Harold Ironhead, and attacked the other party and carried all before him. Thrand asked to make peace with him and offered to stand by the judgment of Earl Hakon. And it is clear enough from the story that Thrand fell into a deep admiration and love for the younger man, and although the judgment of the earl went against him and he lost a great part of his land, yet he was willing to keep the peace for the sake of Sigmund. So now Sigmund sailed back to Norway and married Thurid, the outlaw's daughter, and made peace between Earl Hakon and the outlaw.

So things went on, and Thrand still wanted to be friendly with Sigmund, but Sigmund was still angry against Thrand. Earl Hakon was killed and Olaf the Saint succeeded him; he persuaded Sigmund to be baptised, with his followers. And the next thing was that Sigmund summoned a Thing on the main island of the Faeroes and when a great crowd of people had come Sigmund said, 'I have made a change of faith and become a Christian man. And I have that errand from Olaf the King and his command, to turn all the people of the islands to the right faith.' And he had priests with him, ready to baptise everyone. But Thrand said they must talk this over, and went away with the rest of the landowners to another part of the valley. Here they decided to have nothing to do with this new faith; so for the time it was left like that.

But the next thing was that Sigmund attacked Thrand by night, broke into his house and gave him the choice of baptism or death. At first Thrand said, 'I will not break with my old friends and faith.' But at last he decided to accept baptism and it looks from the story as though he did it in an attempt to get the real friendship of Sigmund. But it does not seem as though Sigmund ever trusted him, whatever he did, or was ever willing to forget and forgive.

The story goes on that King Olaf asked Sigmund to give him Thorgerda Holgabrud's ring in exchange for another as good, since he foresaw that there was danger in the heathen arm-ring. But Sigmund said he could not part with the ring 'for I promised Earl Hakon, when he gave it to me, with so great affection, that I would never give it away'. So Sigmund chose his own luck and went back again to the Faeroes, and built a church. But for all the oaths that might be sworn and for all the men who truly wanted peace, the feud went on, with Thrand, who had never quite forgiven his forcible baptism, and his friends on one side, and on the other Sigmund and Thorir and a man from the Hebrides called Einar. And in the end Thrand and his men attacked Sigmund's house, where Thurid, his wife and mother of half-a-dozen children, 'seized a sword and used it no worse than any hero'. While she held Thrand off, Sigmund, Thorir and Einar got through an underground tunnel to the cliff and leaped down into the sea. Sigmund first tried to help Einar, but he was hurt and died on Sigmund's shoulders, and then Thorir grew too tired to swim. Sigmund held him up for another five miles of swimming, till they came to the southernmost island of the Faeroes, and here Thorir slipped away into the heavy surf and was drowned, but Sigmund was thrown up on to the beach in the first light of dawn. And when it was day, Thorgrim of Sandvik, who held his land from Thrand, came down to the beach and saw the red kirtle in the seaweed. And saw the gold ring on Sigmund's arm. And killed Sigmund, too tired to stand, with his wood axe and took the heathen ring.

Yet the ring brought no luck to Thorgrim and his sons, for Thrand

accused Thorgrim of the murder of Sigmund, and when he denied it
Thrand worked a spell which brought the three ghosts back, dripping
wet, and Sigmund all bloody with his head carried in his hands. And
after that the golden arm-ring was found in the bottom of a great old
chest, and Thorgrim confessed to the murder and was hanged at Thorshaven before the Thing-men. And peace was made.

Thrand must have been an old man by now, but he was not one to
settle down quietly. He seems to have been behind much of the feuding
which still went on. Yet it seemed he was still entangled in some way
between love and hate of the dead man, and he asked to have little
Sigmund, the son of Sigmund's daughter, to foster. The child came to
his house and lived with him from the time he was three years old; he
always slept in the same room as Thrand. But another feud was blowing
up and the child's parents decided to get him back – and this they could
only do by force or trickery, for Thrand, who had no sons of his own,
loved the child deeply. He was nine years old when his mother came
to take him back if she could. First she asked him what Thrand had
taught him. 'He said he had learnt how to carry on a law case and win
his own case against another and how much money he should get for
it.' But when she questioned him on religious instruction, things were
not quite so good. He had his Paternoster right, but his Credo went
rather too much like a heathen rune of protection:

> *I go not out alone.*
> *Four follow me.*
> *God's good angels*
> *Bear my prayers*
> *Before Christ.*
> *I sing seven psalms.*
> *God see to my good fate.*

'I do not think,' said the child's mother to Thrand, 'that I recognise
this Credo.' 'It so happens,' said Thrand, 'that Christ had twelve dis-
ciples or more and each had his Credo. I have my Credo, which is this
one, and there are many credos and not only one right one.'

But after that the parents kidnapped the child, after holing all
Thrand's boats so that he could not follow them; it was not a thing
that was well thought of to take a child away from good fostering. And
a little while afterwards Thrand died of grief. So the story ended and
'it is not told that any other great things happened in the Faeroes'.

All this is told in the Flatey book, which comes into Chapter XII.
There was perhaps some more than life-size quality about the main

people in the story, Thrand and Sigmund, which inspired the teller and then the writer, so that, for a moment, the sharp and shifting light of human significance rested on the small islands in the middle of the sea, before it moved on. The Faeroe island saga is told with superb conciseness; a modern author, given the same material, would have expanded it into one of these huge and boring volumes of regional family fiction.

'IF IT HAD A GOOD NAME'

GREENLAND, like Iceland, was first discovered accidentally, but after that it was rediscovered and settled on purpose. First of all someone called Gunnbjorn sighted some islands off the coast of Greenland, but came back. The islands were named Gunnbjorn-skerries. But nobody knew quite where they were, though later on they came into sailing directions, one man saying they were here, another that they were there.

Then later there is a queer story of some Icelanders: Snaebjorn and Rolf who were outlawed for murder, and their friends, twenty-six men in all, and one or two wives with them. One of these men had a terrible nightmare of foreboding, and they must have sailed hurriedly and in fear, yet knowing that justice would catch up with them if they stayed. Probably few of them had any hope of getting on in the respectable, settled world if they did not go out after their fortunes.

'They went to seek for Gunnbjornskerries and found land. Snaebjorn would not let any one land at night. Styrbjorn went from the ship and found a purse of money in a grave-mound and hid it. Snaebjorn struck at him with an axe and the purse fell. They built a house and covered it all over with snow. Thorkel Raudsson found that the snow had melted on the fork that stuck out at the aperture of the hut. That was in the

month of Goe. Then they dug themselves out. Snaebjorn made ready
the ship. Of his people Thorodd and his wife stayed in the house; and
of Rolf's Styrbjorn and others and the rest went hunting. Styrbjorn
slew Thorodd and both he and Rolf slew Snaebjorn. Raud's sons and
all the others swore faith, in order to save their lives.'

But after that they did not stay in Greenland among their sins. They
came back, and after a time justice did catch up with Rolf and Styrbjorn and that was the end of them. But whose was the purse of money
in the grave mound? Perhaps it was not really a purse of money but a
'treasure', say an Eskimo walrus ivory carving, or some other precious
thing which had been laid with the dead.

We have to ask ourselves how these men had provisioned their ship,
sailing to a country that they were bound to know was inhospitable.
There would have been considerable practice in this, for early settlers
in Iceland must have had their difficulties, as is plain from the story of
Floki who, when he went to explore Iceland, did not bring enough hay
for his cattle so that they all died. They might have to take enough food
for months, good enough for active men to work on. Probably most
of it would be salted meat, but this is not much use by itself. They also
brought live cattle and fodder for them and used the milk. Even in
Greenland there is summer pasture. But were the cows in with the
people in Snaebjorn's house? They would certainly have helped to keep
it warm. If you eat fresh meat, under-cooked, fish – especially fish
livers – and plenty of milk products, you do not get scurvy, even if
there is no fruit and little in the way of vegetables. There is an excellent
modern Shetland dish made of cods' heads and livers which is probably
Norse in origin.

What else did they have? They would have had a certain amount of
meal, but if they started in the spring, meal might have been scarce and
corn would have been scarcer still. But the really bulky thing on board
ship is water. We hear of some ships where everyone got desperate with
thirst. You can't count on rain even in northern waters. We know that
they took casks of water, beer and also whey; the last two would have
added greatly to the vitamin adequacy of their diet.

No doubt they were well prepared for hunting and fishing when they
got to a place. Seals are healthy food, especially in very cold climates,
and the cows would have eaten dried fish, though it would not see
them through the winter unless they had hay as well. The more one
thinks of it, the more highly one rates the courage of the people who
made do and managed not only to survive but to make a civilisation.

4

The real discovery of Greenland was made by a man called Erik the Red, a tough and intelligent man who had come from Norway to Iceland with his father, because they had both got mixed up in a murder. He did not do much better in Iceland. A short time after his marriage, when he had moved to a new part of the country, he had quarrelled with his neighbours and killed several and was made to move on. He seems to have been rather like one of the 'bad men' in a Western. At the next place where he settled, he quarrelled with his neighbours again, this time over the loan of some carved house beams, and killed some of them. Once more he had to leave, outlawed for three years at the session of the Thing at Thorsness.

This must have been in late spring or early summer. He got a ship ready and told his friends – for he seems to have been good at making friends as well as enemies – that he was going to look for Gunnbjorn's islands, and he would come back and tell them if he found them. Among these friends was Thorbiorn, son of Vifil, the Scot-Irish freedman of Aud the Deep-minded. Then Erik set sail, going almost due west, and arrived at the coast of Greenland, at a place where the inland ice does not come right down to the sea, in the way it does along so much of the coast. It must have been a terrifying enough place, that is, if you are the kind of person who can be terrified by the physical world of loneliness, cold, icebergs at sea and enormous glaciers always eating at the narrow edge of summer green, the mosses and grass and thin bright flowers, the scanty willows and birch trees that just survived. But the first land was not possible to live in.

He sailed along the Greenland coast, southward, edging his way through the shifting, dangerous pack ice. Sometimes all would be clear, but always there was the possibility of the ice closing in, nipping and crushing his ship. Inland were bare hills, rising to black mountains, not so inhospitable a coast as that of Iceland, but still not promising for colonists. By the time he rounded Cape Farewell, the southernmost point of Greenland, he would be done with the pack-ice. Perhaps instead he began to feel the mosquitoes, which are bigger and fiercer there than in any other part of the world.

Then he turned north-west, feeling his way up the other side. It must have been a very literal feeling of the way, with no knowledge of what rocks and skerries might be ahead. It was certainly a night-and-day strain on the man in charge of the expedition, who would always be the steersman. Erik the Red would have needed not only sense and courage and quick judgment, but also very good eyesight and great strength to be constantly at the steering oar – rudders were an invention yet to come.

At last they arrived at a more possible looking bit of country, in a way more like the north of Scotland or the mountains and fjords of Norway, Erik's original home. Here there were several miles of country partly covered with grass and bushes and birch trees, which was open in summer between the sea, which, on the western side of Greenland was clear of summer ice, and the inland glaciers. This was what was later to be called the Eastern Settlement.* Erik and his men felt their way in past quantities of small islands and rocks; they had to think of the winter ahead. At last he found a possible place and disembarked and made his winter camp at Erikseye – that is, Erik's Island.

Almost certainly Erik took no cattle with him on his first voyage, though of course he did later on. So the first thing to do would be to build a house of turf and stones, big enough for themselves. Others would be hunting seals, perhaps whales or sea-birds, and fishing, so as to have meat and fish to smoke and dry and salt. These are good fishing grounds still, and in those days must have been wonderful. We do not hear that they met polar bears, but perhaps they would have seen and shot Arctic foxes, less for their flesh than for their skins: they were all able to use a bow and arrows. The ship on which their lives depended must be hauled up very carefully; anything which was loose was brought in and made use of. For instance, the rowers' benches might be unshipped and used as part of the building. The oars, masts and sails and steering oar would be brought in. Also the very necessary water, beer and whey casks. As they had no cattle they probably took a cask or so of sour milk, and probably cheese and salt butter. The sails would curtain off eating and sleeping quarters. The autumn days would hurry by, getting shorter and darker, but even so a little longer than in Iceland, for although it was colder in southern Greenland – because the Gulf Stream turns off to the west before it reaches Greenland – the actual latitude is farther south. We must always remember that it was less cold then than it is now. But no doubt Erik had everything done that could be done before winter.

At the end of the winter he went on north-west, exploring week after week, finding his way up the fjords that wound through the sudden green of spring towards the ice and the dark cliffs and peaks of rock. He would land and make his camp, light a fire of dedication and give a

* It was actually on the west coast; but once one gets so near the Pole, words like east and west get a rather different meaning.

name to the place. It seemed to him at last that this was land which might reasonably be settled and colonised. The second winter he camped again at a place he called Eriksholm; the next summer again he explored north-west and inland into the fjords and viks, landing, putting up marks and giving names. Probably each of his men gave a name to a place. And many of them would be thinking of settling. They seem to have explored most of the Eastern Settlement, going some way up and down the coast and into the winding fjords with the few miles of habitable country at their heads. Then they went up the coast to the part that was to be, later on, the West Settlement. That winter he went back to his original winter quarters.

And now the three years of outlawry were up and he sailed back to Iceland. Almost at once he had a fight with his old enemies and was beaten, but their various friends and neighbours made a settlement between them and they were reconciled and perhaps became friends again. Then Erik called as many people as he could together to go west with him and make a real settlement. He called his new country Greenland, 'because,' said he, 'men would be more willing to go thither if it had a good name'.

He found plenty of people who were only too pleased to try their luck in a new land. It is said that a fleet of twenty-five ships, perhaps more, set sail from Iceland that summer to explore and colonise Greenland, but only fourteen got there. Some were lost and some were driven back, but those that arrived would have men and women and all that they could gather together, beasts and fodder, food and furnishings for a new life. Erik, his wife and children and the rest of the household, settled at Brattahlid, in the East Settlement, and his friends settled all round him, usually naming their holdings after themselves. The people who came out later and found the best land in the East Settlement had been claimed, went on to the West Settlement, made their steadings out of stone and turf and got their farms going. And for a time they made a success of it.

It seems queer that neither in the sagas of Erik the Red nor in any of the other early stories is there any mention of the other inhabitants of Greenland, the Eskimos. There is an occasional mention later on, though usually of deserted houses or boats. Yet these stories of the colonists were mostly written down within the next couple of centuries, some perhaps within a hundred years after the time when the things had actually happened: this would mean that the writers were not too far from speech with, say, the grandchildren of the original settlers.

One would have thought that, if there were Eskimos, something would have been remembered.

Probably the key to it all is climate. The Eskimo civilisation was based on ice-hunting, as indeed it still is, in so far as it has been left unspoilt. Their houses were made of ice blocks and they thought about things like more ingenious ways of spearing seals through holes in the ice. Ice was their familiar climate. So they move with the ice, north or south. Sometimes there is a warm northern spell for several centuries, during which the polar ice shrinks back to the north, and the men and women who live on it move back with it. At the time of the Norse settlement in Greenland, the permanent ice was farther to the north than it is now, and the Eskimos, the original inhabitants, had moved north with it. So for a long time the Norse people and the Eskimos only met on the fringes of their lives, supposing, for instance, an Eskimo boat was disabled and drifted south, or supposing the Norse walrus hunting expeditions went far into the north.

When they are mentioned, it is in no friendly way. The Eskimo were heathen, and heathen they remained. When they were spoken about later in stories of explorers who went beyond the Greenland settlements, or who were wrecked and perhaps rescued, the Eskimos are spoken of as 'trolls'. It was expected that they should behave troll-fashion, that is, that they would normally be the enemies of human beings. They could not speak in any reasonable language. Their clothes were odd. Their weapons were odd. Their food was odd. Their gods were odd. Their magic was odd. In fact they could not be counted as men and women like yourselves. You behaved quite correctly if you just killed them, or if you chopped off the arm of an old 'troll woman', as one of the later explorers did, and so on. Normally they ran away. But if they did not, you were justified in taking any of their belongings. When you were Christian and they were heathen, you were still more justified.

It all depends on what you think of the people who were there before you, when you go out and colonise a new country. Up till very recently we ourselves have been apt to call them 'natives' and think of them with a shade of contempt, and never to consider that it is just possible that the same thing may be said of ourselves some day. The Icelanders said very little about the Celts who were there when they came, in fact they only mention the priests. When Iceland became Christian, people began at once to take an interest in the Christians who had been there at the beginning. It was quite different with the heathen

Eskimo. Nothing was right with them. It made no difference, of course, that there was an Eskimo culture, that they had elaborate art ways and thought ways of their own, built up from their own needs and methods of satisfying them. None of this was realised, nor could it have interested Erik and his friends. Anthropology is a young science, since it conflicted with a number of favourite ideas which people had already. And Erik the Red was no high-brow.

GOLD OF MICKLEGARD

THE Norseman who travelled south would come at last to Constantinople, which was also called Byzantium, as it used to be more than a thousand years before in the days of Alexander, when it was already an important city. But in the mind of the traveller it was Micklegard, greatest of all cities, where the streets were paved with gold.

Constantinople was the gateway to the Middle Sea, the gateway between east and west. Its geographical position was such that it was bound to become rich, apart from being the seat of the most elaborate and powerful court in Europe, perhaps in the world. It had everything, and everyone came there to buy. It was also sacred. It was also terrifying. It had the prestige and wonder of Rome as well as its own riches that constantly flowed in and multiplied themselves. It was also very dangerous, above all to those who aimed high. It was the treasure cave of the Dragon of God and so beyond all alluring to the venturesome man.

How did the venturesome man get there?

He took the East Way, the *austrvegr*, and he went not as a Viking but as a merchant or as a Varangian. That is, he went in peace. He would be trading and perhaps doing some fighting, but usually either to

79

Fine furs for Micklegard

protect himself and other users of the East Way, or else as a soldier of fortune, using his sword's skill as merchandise.

There would be plenty like himself, for the journey took as long as you chose to make it and many a man never reached Micklegard or the Middle Sea or even the Black Sea. He settled down somewhere, married and became involved in the life of another community. This happened most of all in such cities as Novgorod or Kiev, where there would anyhow be many of his fellow-Norsemen. Trade was honourable; it was a dangerous adventure and only to be carried out by a man of courage and intelligence. For long-term success in trading it was also essential to be truthful, so that people would know that your word was as good as your bond. These Varangian traders of the East Way were like the Hudson Bay Company fur traders of the eighteenth and nineteenth century, who travelled along the great waterways of Canada, or the East India Company men whose courage and skill gave them honour among the bravest courts and camps in India.

Most of the East Way men were Swedes, but some were Danes and a few were Norwegians. Let us see how the journey looked from Sweden. A man sailing from one of the ports of eastern Sweden might put in at Gotland or he might sail directly east into the shallow, many islanded Gulf of Finland and land near what is now Leningrad, going on to Lake Ladoga. Here he would turn due south for a hundred miles up the broad, deep Volkhov river which flows into Lake Ilmen. But before he came to Lake Ilmen he would stop at Novgorod which the Norsemen called Holmgard.

This was the city where the nine-year-old King Olaf killed the Viking who had sold him and his mother into slavery. It was so essential that Holmgard should be really a City of Peace that a murder, even a revenge as well justified to most eyes as this, meant death to the murderer. He was only saved by wise Queen Alogia of Novgorod, who managed to persuade the people of Novgorod to accept a money payment for the crime, instead of the boy's life. But we can see why it was necessary in those wild times, when everyone was so free with his axe and sword, to have the strictest possible laws in a crowded trading city; for otherwise the place would have been torn to pieces with bloody riots between one gang of wild foreigners and another.

Novgorod must have seemed a huge place to anyone coming from the clustered villages of Scandinavia, whose king was always on the move, travelling from one big hall to the next, so that there was no real capital city. Even a Viking must have felt himself abashed by its

4*

size and wealth and the crowds in its streets; though it seems as though its fortifications were not as good as those in some of the old cities of the Roman Empire. Novgorod was the first of the new kind of towns in northern Europe. It was essentially a trading city, that is, it had got free from the old ways where you had to fight for everything. For you cannot trade and get rich unless you can trust people. Once someone has killed his creditor instead of paying him the bill and gets away with it, the whole structure is likely to collapse. And it had not, partly because of its geographical isolation, become involved in any feudal system. There were going to be other merchant cities in Europe, the Hansa cities in Germany, Venice and Florence, London itself. Most of them came as a reaction against feudalism. But 'Lord Novgorod the Great' was before them all, though second to the sister city of Kiev in the south and always with close relations between them.

A commercial city does not happen accidentally; it comes where the geographical position is right for certain activities. Novgorod and Kiev, for instance, were both on great waterways, natural places for boats to come in and exchange their cargoes and get water and provisions for the next stage of their journey. A city starts with making travellers pay toll in exchange for food and lodgings, and grows from that.

It is as well to remember that almost all goods went more safely and easily by water until modern times, and even now, when there is an alternative, it is often cheaper and better to send goods by boat rather than by rail and road. In those days there was no rail transport and it was only in the Roman Empire that roads were good enough for wheeled traffic. In places where there were no waterways, goods came by pack animals, horses, mules or camels, or even on the backs of slaves. This meant that they could not go faster than an animal which had to be fed and rested; for unless you used half your pack-beasts to carry fodder for the rest, as well as food for yourself, you had to give them time to graze. They might go lame or die. Above all, they could very easily be attacked and robbed. You had to be prepared to defend them all the time, which meant almost as many armed riders as animals; or else go in a huge caravan with a professional guard.

Water travel was not so difficult and dangerous as that, and cities like Novgorod and Kiev kept a strong and merciless peace on the water-ways. Probably quite a few pirates, water thieves and robbers great and small were hanged and tortured during the year to discourage the rest. It was necessary, otherwise any of the Norsemen, these king's sons out to seek their fortunes, would have thought, here is a fine dragon's hoard for me to rob! But even they were kept in order at Novgorod.

The inhabitants of Novgorod elected or chose themselves a Prince or Leader, but he was always theirs; they were not his. If they did not like him or if they thought he was serving them badly, out he went, and many of the towns would do without a prince for months or years. Queen Alogia, who saved the life of young Olaf, was wife to 'King' Volodimir, but he was only a king so long as he did what the citizens of Novgorod wanted. That is to say, so long as he saw that their laws were kept in full strength and that the city prospered. If a prince did not do what he was told to do, if, for instance, he began to behave as an absolute monarch, or if he began to favour one set of people in the city against another, in a way which was beyond justice, or if he became lazy and did not attend to the defences, then the political machine went into action and out went the Prince of Novgorod. Sometimes he might even be killed or blinded. There were laws which had to be kept and which were gradually being written down (that is, made into a charter) so that they existed as something you could touch and see as well as know in your mind. In Novgorod there was a great bell which summoned the citizens to the meetings where they decided their own destiny and that of their princes.

Each of these great trading cities had the same kind of constitution. They were city-states. This must have been difficult for the Norsemen to understand, but they interpreted what was going on in their own terms. And that is how we hear of the cities in the sagas.

Each city had its citizens' army, and also a certain number of paid soldiers, professionals; these were usually men from Sweden and when we hear about the cities in the sagas we usually hear about them from the point of view of these men. But when we hear about the cities from the Russian point of view, then the professional soldiers, the Varangians, are the foreigners' army. Right at the beginning, some time in the ninth century, the people of Novgorod are said to have called in a Swede called Rurik to keep order and justice and to rule over them. But we know very little about him. He probably existed, but it seems that he really represents a stage when the population of the city-states of Russia had found it was unsatisfactory to go on governing themselves. They wanted someone to take professional charge and save them trouble. What is certain is that the population of the city-states in west Russia was partly Slavonic and partly Swedish and on the whole the Swedes were there as soldiers.

This is the kind of thing that happened; it comes from the Chronicle of Novgorod in the year 1016. Yaroslav was the Prince of Novgorod and he was at war with Svyatapolk who was Prince of Kiev. 'And at that time Yaroslav was keeping many Varangians in Novgorod fearing war; and the Varangians began to commit violence against the wives of the townsmen. The men of Novgorod said: "We cannot look upon this violence," and they gathered by night, and fell upon and killed the Varangians in Poromon's Court; and that night Prince Yaroslav was at Rakomo. And having heard this, Prince Yaroslav was wroth with the townsfolk and gathered a thousand soldiers in Slavno and by craft falling on those who had killed the Varangians he killed them. That same night, Yaroslav's sister, Peredslava, sent word to him from Kiev, saying, "Thy father is dead and thy brethren slain." And having heard this Yaroslav the next day gathered a number of the men of Novgorod and held an Assembly of the People in the open air, and said to them: "I cannot now buy back even with gold my beloved and honourable Druzhina* whom yesterday in my madness I slew." And thus he said to them: "Brethren! My father Volodimir is dead and Svyatapolk is Prince in Kiev: I want to go against him; come with me and help me." And the men of Novgorod said to him: "Yes, Prince, we will follow thee." And he gathered 4,000 soldiers; there were a thousand Varangians and 3,000 of the men of Novgorod; and he went against him.'

After that there was a battle on the banks of the Dneiper against Svyatapolk and his general, Wolf's Tail, which Yaroslav won. 'And Yaroslav went to Kiev and took his seat on the throne of his father Volodimir. And he began to distribute pay to his troops; to the captains ten *grivnas* each, to the common soldiers one *grivna* each, and to all the men of Novgorod ten each, and let them all go to their homes.' A *grivna* was about half a pound of silver, and a mark, the ordinary north European currency, about the same. But sometimes the Varangians were paid in furs or cloth or something of that kind.

Of course, these wars did not go on the whole time. But the Chronicles are like the sagas; they hardly ever record the peaceful and happy years when things go on normally, when the prosperity of the population increases slowly and steadily and everyone can enjoy his or her own life. We all know the saying, 'Happy the land that has no history.' And we who have lived through too much history regard its truth somewhat ruefully. But people who write chronicles and sagas like to have something exciting to write about. Of course, they may get it

* His bodyguard: the citizen-soldiers of Novgorod.

from nature; there might be an eclipse: 'On the 11th day of August before evening service the sun began to decrease and it totally perished; oh, there was great terror and darkness! There were stars and the moon; then it began to reappear and came out quickly in full; then all the city rejoiced.'

Or there might be a famine in which people were driven to eat birch bark and moss and sell their children as slaves. But the good years went by unwritten about and during good years travellers and merchants could go by the East Way unhindered by wars or robbers and see the great cities peacefully and with wonder.

From Novgorod the next stage was south across Lake Ilmen and up the river Lovat. Then there was some kind of way by a canal from the head-waters of the Lovat across the marshes to the head-waters of the river Dneiper, and once the travellers' boat was afloat on the Dneiper it must go south with the current, negotiating the great and dangerous rapids, and after many days down past Kiev to the Black Sea.

Kiev was another great city like Novgorod, built on the low hills above the broad, muddy river; and it was a very beautiful one. There was surplus money about in the trading cities and much of it was used to build churches with painted walls and painted domes, monasteries and rambling palaces or public buildings. We hear about Kiev from the other end, from the historians of the Byzantine Empire, who thought of it as a home of wicked and cruel barbarians who periodically came south to raid and hold up to ransom the civilised inhabitants of the Empire. The first invasion from Kiev was in the ninth century and the same thing happened as had been happening in the west, where first the old Roman Empire and then Charlemagne's Holy Roman Empire broke up and were attacked by barbarian invaders, Vikings and others. In the east too, whenever the frontiers were weakened by internal wars and disputes – sometimes over religion – the barbarians attacked.

Through marshes and a wide delta the Dneiper flows down into the Black Sea. The people here were probably Magyars, still wandering, making their way gradually westward towards Hungary, with their covered wagons and great herds of horses and cattle. I think there must have been a town on the Dneiper delta where the river boats were exchanged for sea-going craft, perhaps the remains of the old Greek settlement of Olbia. The Black Sea, beautiful as it looks, can be wild and treacherous. The sea-going craft must dodge along the shore, putting in here and there at ports where Greek would be the language spoken and Greekish clothes would be worn, long tunics and sandals instead of short kirtle and breeches. And here the traveller would get news of what was happening at Micklegard and what kind of welcome he might get. He would know that if he came to trade, he must go unarmed, with a safe conduct from the ruler of his last place of stay. He must promise peaceful behaviour, would not be allowed to buy goods above a certain price and quality, which must be marked by an official, but then could lodge, free – presumably in some kind of cara-vanserai – for a period up to six months in the suburb of Saint Mamas.

If he came with a sword to sell, he would no doubt get in touch with his fellow-countrymen in the Varangian court. Indeed he might have been specifically recruited for that in his own country. The Varangians were just as much needed by the emperors of Micklegard as they were by the princes of the Russian cities, and on the whole the emperors paid better. So by the tenth century there was a Varangian Palace Guard at Constantinople and many a brave man made his fortune there. One of them was Harald Hardrada (that is to say, the hard counsellor), the stepbrother of King Olaf the Saint, the man who nearly won England but was killed at the battle of Stamford Bridge. It was very useful for him to have so near a relative in heaven, and Saint Olaf seems to have done one or two miracles for him.

Harald had to leave Norway after the battle where King Olaf was killed. He went first to Holmgard – Novgorod – and stayed some years as captain of Prince Yaroslav's Varangians. I do not think he could have been there at the time of the story I have just quoted from the Chronicles of Novgorod, but possibly soon after. Here he was betrothed to Elizabeth, or Ellisif (like the Gaelic Ealasaid), the Prince's daughter. Yaroslav was more than an elected Prince; after his victory over Svyatapolk, he became Prince of Kiev and all the waterways and all the cattle and all the smaller towns between. He married off his children wherever they might help him to keep the peace. One son married a Princess of Constantinople and another a daughter of Harold of England, and his own daughters all became queens.

But after a time Harald thought he would go on to Micklegard, so he went with a great company of men and took service with the Empress Zoe. There was great jealousy between his army and the Greek army and as often as not they came to fighting. But the Varangians were so necessary as a Palace Guard, that the empress always tried to make up the quarrels and bribed the Varangians to stay. Harald was a great warrior and his men were always taking spoil, but he sent his back to Prince Yaroslav, his future father-in-law, who took care of it for him. 'He had so much wealth as no man in the North lands had seen in one man's holding.' But it was not only from the cities that he took his gold. He was lucky in another way. Harald had three times come into palace spoil while he was in Micklegard. 'For the law is that whenever the Emperor of the Greeks dies, the Varangians shall have palace spoil. They shall go over all the Emperor's palaces where are his treasures, and there each one shall freely have for his own everything he may lay hands on.'

This, at any rate, is what it says in the sagas, but it seems unlikely that it was an official Byzantine law! It is much more likely to have been a custom which the Varangians managed sometimes to insist on. The Empress Zoe had several husbands and one or two came to untimely ends, as happened often enough in the emperor's palace.

Harald took towns in North Africa and Sicily, using all kinds of craft. For instance, he tied shavings dipped in sulphur on to the backs of birds which nested in one town, so that the thatch caught fire. In another place they dug underneath the wall of the town into a hall where the townspeople were sitting and the Varangians burst through, killed some and took the town. In another he is said to have used the same craft as Hasting had done earlier on and pretended to be dead, so that he and his men could get into the cathedral.

However, there was one land which he visited in peace; this was Palestine. He went as a pilgrim to Jerusalem and neither burnt nor harried. He swam in the Jordan and perhaps, like a later King of Norway, tied lucky knots in the bushes at the side of the river. And he gave much gold to the churches of Jerusalem which held the holiest relics. Here he would have found many other travellers besides himself, men, and even women, among them the noblest, from all parts of western civilisation. The crusades were yet to come – meantime pilgrims could come and go in peace, to be blest in the places of their deepest dream and faith and for a time to become better people.

Some might buy relics, genuine or not, and carry them back to cathedrals or little village churches, utterly remote from the hot suns and bright colours of Palestine. Men who had killed their neighbours in a feud – common enough in the Norse countries and Iceland – widows whose sons and daughters were settled and who could at last do what they had long set their hearts on: all came as pilgrims, mostly to Rome, but sometimes on to Palestine. All tongues of Europe were spoken in Jerusalem, and all at peace. Constantly, throughout all sagas and

MAP 2

adoga

GOROD (Holmgard)

en

at

R. Don

V

R. Dnieper

To ASTRAKHAN

To SAMARKAND

TREBIZOND

KLEGARD
(Byzantium)

chronicles we hear of these pilgrims and often their journey is described in detail.

There were, for instance, the two tenth-century Icelanders, Thorvald, Codran's son, who was disliked by his father and brought up by a spae-wife, who advised him to travel, and Stephen Thorgil's son. 'They travelled together far and wide over the world, and all the way out to Jersualem: and thence to Micklegard and so on to Coenugard east along the Dnieper'. Now, Coenugard is probably the modern Kovno, on the Nyemen. The head-waters of the Dnieper and Nyemen might have had a canal joining them, or else there was a land portage; but in Iceland, where the story was written down, you thought of them all as being part of one great river. After that Thorvald died in Russia a short way from Palteskia. This must have been Polotsk on the Dvina, another river with its head-waters in the same enormous marsh-land which feeds the great rivers of central and eastern Europe. There Thorvald the Icelander 'is buried in a certain hill at the church of John the Baptist, and they call him a saint. So saith Brand the Far-farer:

> *I have been where to Thorvald*
> *Codran's son Christ gives rest.*
> *He is buried in a high hill*
> *Up on the Dnieper at John's Church.'*

Not having a geographically critical audience, Brand the Far-farer calls the Dvina the Dnieper. On the other hand it may be that Polotsk is wrong and that really the Icelander was buried in the great hill-Monastery at Kiev. Brand himself must have done a great deal of travelling before he got that nickname.

Stephen Thorgil's son went on to Denmark. There he got into trouble with one of the earls, who killed him.

But these were just two of the travellers who came to Jerusalem. They were from the first generation of Christian converts in Iceland – two, I think, who took the whole thing very seriously and felt it laid upon them to go to the Holy Places. Perhaps some of their friends and relations were still heathen or only nominally Christian, and Stephen and Thorvald may have felt that if they went on this pilgrimage they would be a kind of sacrifice for the others. When Harald went to Jerusalem he must have met and spoken with many pilgrims such as those. Probably he was generous and hospitable to them, and some of them might have news from home. Indeed it might have been pilgrim's news that decided him to leave Micklegard and his conquests and go home again.

In the last month of Harald Hardrada's stay, there is a story of his love for the Empress Zoe's niece, Maria; and of how the empress herself disapproved of it and imprisoned Harald, but he escaped with the help of his stepbrother, Saint Olaf, who worked a small miracle for him, and carried off Maria in his galley. The empress had chains thrown across the mouth of the harbour, but they rowed their galleys hard at them, ran them on and then all rushed forward, so that one galley tipped off the chain safely on to the far side, though the other broke her back on the chain and was lost. However, Harald escaped successfully, put Maria ashore with an escort and sent her back to the empress, with a message saying he would do as he pleased.

So then he sailed back through the Black Sea and north again, and on his way he made up a song about Yaroslav's daughter Elizabeth, and each verse with the same ending, something like this:

> And still the gold-ringed lassie
> Laughs light at all my ventures,
> The gold-ringed lass of Holmgard!

That winter he and Elizabeth were married and the year after he went back to Scandinavia. Here he found King Magnus, the son of King Olaf the Saint, who was not entirely pleased at the return of his terrible stepuncle. But they made peace and divided the kingdom. Then they feasted, and an oxhide and a number of bags were brought into the tent. King Harald spoke to King Magnus, saying, 'You gave me half the kingdom which you had won from our enemies and you took me into fellowship. This was well done. But I have lived in exile and it has cost many dangers to bring together this gold which you now see. I will lay it down in fellowship with you for we shall own our goods equally, just as we each own half the kingdom of Norway.' Then Harald poured the gold from the bags on to the cowhide and it was shared by weight: 'And all who saw it thought it a great wonder that in the northlands so much gold should be come together in one place. But indeed this was the treasure of the Emperor of the Greeks in whose city as all men say, houses are full of red gold.'

And now I think we must reluctantly remind ourselves that perhaps Harald Hardrada was not only a good fighter and an efficient treasure gatherer, but also an excellent story-teller. And who was to check up on his or his friends' stories of what had happened in Micklegard? His own men would back him up, for their honour and glory were involved too. And it is not much good looking elsewhere. From Byzantine sources, we find very little about the Varangians, except that they were a useful but sometimes dangerous palace guard. However, that is not necessarily the whole truth. The Byzantine chroniclers would want to give all the credit for victories to their own generals, just as the saga-writers wanted to give all the credit to Harald and his friends.

This only shows you that you must never trust historians! They always want to prove something. They have some particular point of view and anything they write about is given a little twist towards it; they pick out the facts which show up whatever they want people to believe. Of course, in a very remote historical period about which very little is known, it may be just possible to write down every single one of the facts, and to do it in such a way that readers can draw no particular conclusions from them. But it would be a very, very dull book.

But there was a long and highly coloured life yet for Harald Hardrada, with plenty of battles and raiding and gold and dragon-ships, and another wife, Thora, Thorberg Arnison's daughter, whose two sons succeeded him as Kings of Norway after his death in England. Harald had become sole king after the death of Magnus; he was tough and clever and a good leader. And he was a friend to the Iceland folk and once, when they were short of food, he sent four ships loaded with meal to Iceland with orders that it should be sold at a reasonable price, and he also sent a bell for the church in Iceland for which his brother the Saint had sent the wood. And indeed there is plenty about Saint Olaf and his miracles in the saga of Harald Hardrada.

The main war was always with King Svein of Denmark, until at last they were induced to make peace with one another. And soon after that Earl Tosti, the brother of our own King Harold Godwinsson, came to Norway to persuade King Harald Hardrada to invade England, which was the kind of ploy to appeal greatly to someone who was for the moment at peace. So, when he had made up his mind to the invasion of England, Harald Hardrada cut his hair and nails and offered them at the shrine of his half-brother, and he gathered his host, two hundred great ships and many smaller. He left his son Magnus as king in his stead in Norway, and his mother Thora, Thorberg's daughter, with him. But he took Queen Ellisif and her daughters Maria and Ingigerd, sailing and picking up reinforcements in Shetland and the Orkneys, where he left the ladies to wait for him.

But long, long must they wait, with the gold combs in their hands. For Harald Hardrada sailed south, burning Scarborough on his way, and landed near Stamford Bridge. His brother-in-law, Eystein Heathcock, the son of Thorberg, the Earls of Orkney and Harald's younger son Olaf were guarding the ships, and it was hot weather and all were in good heart. But in a while they saw a cloud of dust coming up from the south, 'and nearer that host drew, the more it was, and all like an ice heap with the glint of weapons'.

So then King Harald Hardrada set up his banner Landwaster and saw to the marshalling of his men, for he knew it would be a very fierce and hard fight. He was on a black-blazed horse and the horse fell and the king off him. Yet he jumped to his feet quickly saying, 'Fall is faring-luck.' But Harold Godwinsson, watching the other king, said: 'A big man, and masterful; but perhaps his luck is out.'

And so indeed it was, for King Harald Hardrada fell with an arrow through his throat and his host was beaten back to the sea. And on the same day and at the same hour his daughter Maria died in the Orkneys 'and it is said that they had but one life'. Yet the luck was out too for Harold Godwinsson, for the wind shifted that let William of Normandy across the Channel and nineteen days after the Battle of Stamford Bridge came the battle of Hastings and all that followed from it.

Hold still, Biorn!

TRAVEL BY FORCE
OR BY CHOICE

THIS same Harald Hardrada comes into plenty of stories; he was the kind of man who impressed himself on the imagination of his time. He is the villain and causer of exile in the story of Heming, and you can recognise him as the man who, when he was a Varangian captain, is said to have been the one to gouge out the eyes of the usurping emperor Michael V.

The story of Heming starts with Harald leaving a skin 'flayed from the biggest he-goat, full of gold and pure silver' with Ellisif, the lass of Holmgard. It then goes on to speak of his followers, including various Icelanders, among them one Odd, Ofeig's son. They went around, holding courts and feasting here and there, something of a burden for those who had to give provisions for man and beast. At the house of Aslak of Torgir, the king accused his host of bringing up a son in secret and demanded that the boy should be brought to him. After doing his best to get out of it, for there seemed to be something ill-omened about the demand, Aslak finally sent for his son Heming who had been brought up secretly and who was so skilful and strong that he could do all feats of sport or warfare better than any other man in Norway. The king began to challenge him and got more and more angry as Heming beat him in shooting, both with arrow and spear. He made Heming shoot a nut off the head of his brother Biorn, and the Icelander Odd was the one who watched to see that it was hit.

Next was the swimming challenge. It ended with Heming helping back to shore the man whom the king had sent to beat him at this sport – it seems as though the Norsemen were all great swimmers. Then Harald Hardrada himself challenged Heming, throwing off his clothes and plunging in, pulling Heming, tired from his first swim, under water among rough waves. It began to grow dark and the king struck out for land and put on his clothes, alone. 'There was little merriment.' The king was dumb and furious, Aslak deeply grieved for his son. 'Fires were lit in the hall. When all had taken their seats Heming walks into the hall before the king and lays a strap-knife on his knee which the king had on his neck when he plunged out swimming. All thought they knew that he must have taken the knife.' And that the king had meant to stab him treacherously in the water.

Then came the test on snow-shoes, which must have been some kind of ski, not the Canadian type of real snow-shoe. They were all on the edge of a cliff, and finally the king bade Heming come down the slope and stop at the cliff's edge beside him. It was clear that nothing would satisfy the king but Heming's death. Aslak offered all his property if his son could get peace, but the king would not have it. Then the Icelander Odd gave him a linen cloth, a relic of Saint Stephen, and if it saved him he asked Heming to take good care of it. The king was wearing a red kirtle and a scarlet cloak over it. He loosened the straps of the cloak and stood near the cliff's edge. Then Heming came down the hill. 'He shook off the straps of his snow-shoes and sprang up into the air, and the snow-shoes went gliding over but he came down on his feet at the very edge. He swayed about: and clutched at the king's cloak, but the king bowed down his head and the cloak stripped off. Then Heming slipped down over the cliff.'

Odd the Icelander told the king exactly what he thought of him and Harald told the rest to take Odd and throw him over the cliff to join Heming. But Halldor, another Icelander answered: 'Either all we Icelanders who are here now will die together or none of us: but we will have something to show for our lives.' So the king gave Odd peace for that winter, and Odd left him and went back to Iceland.

But meanwhile Heming had been caught on a jag of the cliff by a corner of the linen cloth, the relic of Saint Stephen. When Heming came to from his fall he made a vow to share all his goods in three parts, a third to King Olaf the Saint, a third to pilgrims and poor men, and the other third to Saint Stephen – but that he would give to Odd. He himself would go on a pilgrimage to Rome. And lastly he prayed 'that I may stand as close to King Harald's death as he now thought he was to my death'. Then it seemed as though there was a great light and someone walked down the crag face, and this was Saint Olaf, Harald's stepbrother, come to help him, 'for I would not,' said the saint, 'that thou wert lost and King Harald's guilt increased . . . thou shalt be close by when King Harald dies; but thou shalt ill repay me if thou takest much part in that quarrel'. And then it seemed that the vision faded, but a boat was lying in below and he rowed out to Torgir. Here he found his father and brother praying for him among lighted tapers in the church. 'They were more glad than tongue can tell.' Heming stayed hidden over the winter, but in spring he shared his goods, according to his vow, and sailed for England, taking Saint Stephen's third, which he had not yet been able to give back to Odd. He left it in safe keeping in London – where? – perhaps with a church? – and went south to Rome.

When he came back he stayed, under an assumed name – as he had been warned to do in the vision by Saint Olaf – at the court of Edward the Confessor, and sent word to Odd in Iceland. So Odd fitted out his ship and sailed by way of the Orkneys, and round to London, where he stayed that winter. He had two bells cast; Heming begged him to build a church for the housing of the relic. There is a story of how at the king's court, Odd met a Viking who had killed his brother and taken his cloak and sword; his name was Adalbright, which sounds Frisian or Norman. When he said he had bought the things, Odd threatened him with a stroke from King Edward's magic sword, Touchtine, which would only bite on liars. The man confessed and paid Odd a hundred marks of silver as blood fine, and Odd sailed off. He was driven by weather to Norway and nearly caught by King Harald – for of course Odd was still an outlaw in Norway. But the protection of the relic held and they got it back safe to Iceland and built a church. The cloth was still there in the late sixteenth century.

Saxon London must have been a tremendously lively little capital, packed with people between its walls, vulnerable from the Thames, but there would be look-outs farther down to signal back if boats looked unfriendly. But there would be plenty of merchant ships and visitors come to get and spend money. The ox-carts would come in from the countryside bringing food to market; there would always be a price to be got in London. And it was not far for Londoners to walk or ride out into the woods for their sport. The tidal Thames acted as a drain, and with London still reasonably small that was good enough, and it could have been a healthy and pleasant town. Those were the days when Edward asked young Harold, Earl Godwin's son, to come to his court. Heming taught Harold all his games and feats of strength and Harold was the only man in England who knew all about him.

So time went on until the battle of Stamford Bridge, and here, it says in the story, Heming was at the side of Harold Godwinsson. Now it mattered very much to each side to pick out and kill the leaders on the other, and Harold Godwinsson bade Heming be sure to shoot the Norwegian king, for he alone among the English would know Harald Hardrada for certain. 'I have marked down the king,' said Heming, 'but I dare not shoot him because of Saint Olaf.' 'Shoot so that I know him,' said our King Harold, for he was under no obligation to Saint Olaf. So Heming shot Harald Hardrada with a kind of light arrow with a loose point, used for marking, and when that was done Harold Godwinsson shot him in the throat, and he died.

But after that the same kind of thing happened, for Tosti Godwinsson was now leading, and Harold would not be the one to kill his brother. So it was Heming who shot Earl Tosti. 'This marked me for God,' said Tosti and he died.

And after that the story goes on to the hard and sad battle of Hastings. It tells a story which must have had some currency, of how King Harold was taken off the field, wounded, by two poor folk and hidden at risk of their lives and healed. Heming was told, came to the king and offered to go through the land and gather a host and turn William out. But the king refused; there would be too much death and oath-breaking. His mind was on the pattern of Olaf the Saint. He went into a hermit's cell at Canterbury where from time to time he would see King William in the church. And after three years he died. Then Heming told King William, and William at first would have killed him, but then offered to make him the foremost baron in the land if he would serve him as he had served Harold Godwinsson. But Heming said he had no more wish for money or power, but he would like to go to the same cell and spend his days there. 'The king was silent for a long time and then said: "For that this is asked of a clean heart, then shall it be granted thee."' And so it was, and Heming served God in Canterbury until his old age, and died there.

It is said in another story that many of the English, who could not bear to live under King William, sailed round Spain and through the Straits, plundering as they went. Here they heard of the siege of

Constantinople under Alexis I, whom they called Kiralax the Tall. 'When the English heard of strife out of Micklegarth they looked for great advancement.' So they sailed east and came by night to the city 'and ran into battle at once against those who lay on ship-board' and beat them off – or so they said. The emperor 'took wonderfully well to them' and asked them to join the Varangian guard. But some of them thought it was not enough of a career, and they would like to conquer some land for themselves. So they went to a land which lies 'six days and nights sail east and north east of Micklegard; there is the best of land there'. They conquered it, drove out the inhabitants, called the country England, and called the towns in it London and York and so on. One wonders if this was the Crimea or the Kuban district. Perhaps one day something will be found which will tell us.

The Mediterranean must have had its share of northern pirates, respectable Christians perhaps in their own country. There was Earl Rognvald of Orkney who set sail with fifteen large ships, commanded by Orkney nobles, including William the Bishop, coasting down the east of England with an eye open, no doubt for anything that could be got – but folk would be on their guard. They had pleasant adventures in northern France, especially with a beautiful young queen who feasted him (perhaps a wise way of dealing with a strong and possibly hostile force) and whom he promised to come back and marry, but somehow never did. They went the usual way, stopping to plunder and burn in Spain; at that time Spain was half Moslem, so there was plenty of excuse.

In the Mediterranean they attacked a *dromund*, one of the great Saracen ships, armed with Greek fire and blazing pitch; the description of the fight sounds oddly like one of the battles five centuries later between the little English ships and the great ships of the Spanish Armada. Some of the little ships ran in under the curving sides and bow of the *dromund*, while others shot arrows from a distance. The men in the small boats, some standing on the flukes of the *dromund*'s anchor, hacked away at the planks and managed to make a hole large enough to get through. So they boarded the ship and fought fiercely from the lower deck to the upper, at last capturing the ship, getting great booty, but failing to find all the treasure, which melted away and flowed into the sea when in the end they fired the *dromund*.

They put into Sicily and sold part of their booty and prisoners and then went on to Crete where they anchored off the land. By this time no doubt they had talked it all over, who had been foremost, where

the greatest honour lay and had agreed that 'everyone should afterwards tell the story in the same way that Earl Rognvald did'. Meanwhile one man or another was making up songs, which were duly set
down.

From Crete they sailed to Acre, where some of them died; they
made their pilgrimages to all the holy places. Then they went to some
city where one of them who was very drunk, seems to have fallen into
the main drain, and another was murdered. Finally they got to Micklegard on a fair wind, making their ships look splendidly, and spent most
of the winter there, with the Emperor Manuel. They left some of the
ships, and the earl, the bishop and some others, rode by horse to Rome
and then north-east across Europe to Denmark and then to Norway,
getting great honour, since by the end they had travelled farther and
on more routes than any men of their time. Travel itself was an honourable and wonderful thing and they would now have stories enough to
last the rest of their lives.

These folk brought back money and silver from their wanderings,
and it turns up duly stamped with the stiff little Byzantine emblems,
in hoards and treasures all over the Norse land. No doubt too they
brought back the latest Micklegard fashions, both of dress, government
and religion, if not to adopt, at least to talk about. They never seem to
have managed to find out about Greek fire, but that was top secret.
The dragon of Byzantium was curled well and truly about such matters.

WAYS OUT OF DENMARK

THE main East Way from Sweden to the south has been described in Chapter IX. But there was yet another way of going east and then south. This was by another great river, the Oder. It was the Danish way. It missed out Holmgard, but it connected up farther south, and at the end lay the same glittering Micklegard. It was never quite as important a water-way as the other, but many travellers must have used it in their time.

But, like the other water-way, it had to be guarded. And it seems that, in the tenth century, Blue-Tooth Harald, the King of Denmark, encouraged the Danish Vikings to set up a city of their own to guard the mouth of the Oder against other Vikings and to let the ordinary merchant or traveller go by in peace. Conceivably these were subjects of his whom he was glad to get rid of. If a Danish traveller wanted to get to Micklegard, he could voyage up the Oder and cross eastwards into the Vistula and again work upstream against the slow current into the Pripet Marshes and across there to the head-waters of the Dneiper tributaries which would take him south past Kiev and into the main water-way. When we think of the crossing from the head-waters of one river into those of another, we should remember that there may well have been water-ways, secret Swan Roads through rush and reed, which have been lost and bogged over for centuries now. There is a large, flat, sandy island in the mouth of the Oder and it became the trade centre and meeting place for merchants. But all was guarded by the fortress city of Jomsburg, held by the Jomsvikings, who were something like the Orders of Knights in the crusading days later on. They were bound by strict oaths of fidelity and courage. Everything they had was owned in common. Each Viking, none younger than eighteen and none older than fifty, was tested in combat with two other men each as well armed as he was. They were not allowed outside the fortress without permission for more than three nights. No woman was allowed inside their fortress. Anyone who broke the rules was expelled.

To begin with most of them were Danish, but there were thousands of men who came to join them, men whose lives had been thwarted in some way, men who wanted to be part of so noble and notorious a community. Most likely they came from all the countries where there had been Viking raids and where a Viking way of life was known about. There may well have been English, Scots, Irish, and Welsh – Britons – among them. Some of them knew the hot sun of the Mediterranean and the edges of the African desert. But now they had found another fate. Dasent wrote a story about them called 'Vikings of the Baltic', most of which comes from their own special saga. The fortress of Jomsburg was thought to be impregnable. Three hundred ships could lie safe in its gated harbour. Here they wintered and in summer they went out raiding.

So it went on for two or three generations, and then came war with Norway. There was a fearful battle with portents and appearances and a storm of huge hailstones. No quarter was asked or given. One of the Jomsburg leaders, Bui the Thick, was badly wounded and his ship likely to be captured. He caught up two heavy chests of gold, 'and shouted, "Overboard all Bui's men!" And himself leaped overboard with the chests and sank, and with that many men of his leapt overboard and others were killed on the ship, for there was no use of them asking for peace. So was Bui's ship cleared from stem to stern and then the rest of the ships one after another.'

Some of the Jomsvikings were captured and bound together with a long rope. They sat along a tree trunk and now was their chance to show that their courage was different from that of all other men. Each gave a good answer before he was killed and upheld the fame of his fortress. One of them showed a scientific interest, saying that it had never been proved whether a man could feel anything when his head was off; so if he himself could feel anything, he would thrust the cloak pin which he held in his hand into the earth. But when his head was cut off, the hand only dropped the pin. Near him was one of the young Vikings who had very beautiful long fair hair; he asked that it should not be spoiled and pulled it up over his head and gave it to one of the Norwegians to hold. But just as the axe came down, the young Viking pulled back his head and the axe came down on the hands of the man who was holding his hair and took them off. Now this was the kind of practical joke which always appealed to Norsemen and it was so much appreciated that one of the Norwegian earls insisted on giving peace to this lad, although he was a son of Bui's, and to his friends.

This battle broke the power of the Jomsvikings for a time, but they were not rooted out until the middle of the eleventh century. Perhaps while they held Jomsburg, Danish merchants and travellers went safe, and certainly there was great trade between Denmark and the east or south. We can tell this from the hoards of gold and silver, including many coins from Constantinople and some from even farther east, which prove that there was some kind of contact, even as far as the Caspian Sea and Arabia. You could get to the Caspian Sea down the river Volga, and there was some kind of connection, perhaps by canal, perhaps by a short overland carry, between the head-waters of the Volga and the ordinary Ladoga–Ilmen route. Once you got to the Caspian you were on one of the main routes to the east, and Chinese silk for Danish ladies. So the Jomsvikings may have protected the Danish merchants and travellers and may have frightened all other robbers and pirates from the lower waters of the Oder. But probably there were other travellers by the East Way who were deeply relieved to hear that the Jomsvikings were no more.

Nothing has actually been found in modern times which corresponds to Jomsburg. But it is possible that this may happen yet. Nobody is quite certain of the exact site and in ten centuries or so a place may disappear, stone be taken away – at any rate in a country where building stone is scarce – wood and plaster rot into dust and mud, and earthworks gradually work down to land level. Or the course of a river may alter and everything be washed away.

But something else has been found. This is a Viking fortress which must have been as large as Jomsburg or even larger and about which there is no history, no saga, no remembrance at all. It is the fortress of Trelleborg on the main island of Denmark close to the Great Belt. In fact at the time it was used, the waters of the Great Belt came inland here in a long, shallow sea loch, half surrounding the fortress. Several hundred boats might have lain at anchor just off the walls where now the red Danish cows graze on soft-bottomed pasture.

Trelleborg has been very well excavated in the last few years. New methods have been used and the result shows a double earth-ringed fortress big enough to hold perhaps two thousand men. In the inner ring, spaced out with mathematical precision, are four groups of houses, each group consisting of four houses at the four sides of a courtyard. There is a symmetry about this and about the perfect right-angles at which the roads between these four blocks go, which suggests immediately that the builders of the camp had been influenced by Roman camp building, and the Roman foot appears to be the standard of measurement used. Now the puzzle begins. Had the architects and engineers of this fortress travelled and taken notes? Or were they using Roman or Byzantine text-books and diagrams? – in which case it is a little odd that nothing of the kind from this date has survived in the northern world. One thing is certain: they no longer thought of Roman civilisation in terms of dragons and gold hoards; they had got a stage beyond that.

There is one other place where they might have got this kind of knowledge, and that was England. Alfred the Great had decided quite deliberately that the English must learn as much as possible from Rome and Byzantium. They must stop being barbarians. He had sent people to find out and had had books copied. Others had carried on this tradition. It is quite possible that these Danes got their knowledge of Roman methods of engineering and building from their cousins in the Danemark of England, who had in turn got them from the English. They might have brought engineers or surveyors with them, perhaps as captives, but much more likely as highly paid and honoured guests.

Yet the typical Roman camp is square; this, though divided into quarters, is set in a circle. There are camps of this kind east of Byzantium. I am inclined to think we underestimate the effects of the various ancient civilisations on one another. True, they did not have our means of communication without which we feel ourselves lost; there was no printing, no railways and aeroplanes. But people travelled and used their eyes. One of the functions of any royal court was to be a kind of hotel. A man who lived up to certain standards of 'civilised' behaviour could assume some kind of welcome and would be able to pay for it in news and gossip, just as the travelling tinkers did in the Highlands before the days of newspapers. There is constant mention of foreigners in the various Byzantine chronicles; no doubt something of the same kind went on across the whole Iranian world, perhaps as far as China. So long as the guest was prepared to conform with the customs, manners and religion of his hosts, everything went well. If a man came from so far off that he was obviously no danger, he would be allowed to look at the latest fortresses and armouries – though there were always some secrets, such as Greek fire, which would be well guarded. Trelleborg, then, may have had its origin in the Mediterranean or even farther.

But there is something even odder than the use of Roman standards of measurement about these squares of houses. Each house is shaped like a ship cut off each end at bow and stern, divided internally into a large hold or living-room, and two smaller rooms, forward and aft. There appears to be an open gallery or veranda running all round, though there is now some dispute about this, and of course a hearth in the middle of each living-room. Each house was of such a size that it would hold between seventy and eighty men: a ship's crew?

Now it may be that these houses were not deliberately ship-shaped. At present they look like it – one sees the foundations very clearly because the holes where the timbers used to be showed up very clearly in the soil and have since been filled in with concrete. When I was there I could not help seeing each square of houses as four ships tied up bow and stern in a possible defensive position. Outside the inner fortress ring, but within the outer ring, are quite a number more of these ship houses but all built radially, exactly like ships tied up to a buoy.

It is also, I suppose, possible that these houses were originally roofed with old boats, but I rather doubt it. They seem too deliberately planned for that, besides they are not the shape of a Viking long-ship but rather of a round-ship or trading ship. Yet it may also be that they are ship-shaped simply because the bulge out in the living-room enables more men to live in each house, to gather round the central hearth and sleep on the wide benches all along the walls, than in an ordinary straight-sided house. But the curved house is far more difficult to build. The walls are on a regular ellipse which could hardly have been drawn out free-hand – even by a boat-builder. For that matter, would either the Viking ships or the trading ships have been built without plans or drawings of some kind? It may be they could have been built from small wooden models, shaped with a sharp knife, but few boat-builders now would care to undertake such a thing. We are left with a mass of questions and perhaps a sense of annoyance that history is so much about battles and kings and so little about details of things like building.

5

For instance, at Trelleborg, was the gallery round the house used for storing ships' gear which need not be under cover during winter? If the houses were not roofed with boats, were they roofed with wooden shingles as was done on the model house that Danish architects have built just outside the fortifications? Or were they thatched with the local rushes? It is possible to estimate the amount of timber used; this would have meant the felling of some eight thousand large trees, mostly oaks but probably some pines and lime trees, perhaps two hundred acres of forest. Most of the trees were then cut up, probably split with axes and wedges into broad and heavy planks, two to three inches thick, each of which would need several men to handle it. In addition to the houses and store-houses, there were duck-board roads laid on piles all about the camp. You would need that for several thousand men in a winter camp. But consider the labour force involved! The phosphate content of the soil in this and other camps is still very high; one can imagine what they smelled like when they were in use.

I also wish I knew what used to happen in the squares inside the four blocks of houses. I may be quite wrong, but I had an uneasy feeling that discipline amounting to cruelty was practised there. It seemed to me that it would be remarkably unpleasant to be a prisoner in that camp. Nor is it likely that there would be any women of the status of wives. In fact I got a feeling of something rather like Nazi-ism out of Trelleborg. But I may be wrong; this is only a personal impression.

Only one thing is quite plain. These Vikings were not amateurs, but professionals. They were highly organised and could command, not only supplies, but also the services of skilled engineers. They must have had the backing of the central power in the country in which they lived.

Archaeological evidence points to a date in the tenth or eleventh century, possibly under King Svend of the Forked Beard, son of Blue-Tooth Harald. The population of Denmark had grown very much and the land could not produce enough food for everyone. It was essential to get a good number of the young men away, preferably in a community without marriage and increase of population. It seems likely that Trelleborg was deliberately organised and built at the king's orders. In the last few years, since Trelleborg was excavated, two other Viking camps have been found. One of them, Aggersborg, is mentioned by Saxo. King Kanute took refuge there for a couple of nights. There is a third, smaller one, built in much the same situation as Trelleborg, in a marsh with a burn round it: it has only a modern name. All three camps are built on the same system. It is possible that there may have been others which have completely disappeared, though there is always a chance that, with the use of new archaeological methods in the hands of capable and enthusiastic Danish archaeologists, more will be discovered. But even three would have meant a great number of men under arms. Supposing they decided not to owe allegiance to the king? Or to throw in their weight on one side or another in a dynastic struggle? They must have needed very tactful handling, to say the least.

But I think one can assume that it was from camps like these that some, perhaps most, of the Viking raids went out, after a winter of tough military training, I expect. The long serpents would glide out with even strike of oars. Once in the Great Belt up would go the red or striped sails; they would pass north between Jylland and Sweden; they would round the Skaw and so into the fierce currents of the Kattegat. And a few days later some country, perhaps our own, would be battered by the invasion of a Viking fleet.

Half England was under the Danes, as we know, as well as what is now the German coast. The long serpents might have headed due west or turned south. From places like Trelleborg they may have gone out against all the coasts of Europe. They brought back riches; some of them settled; they had great possessions. Songs must have been made up about them, stories told. But, as things chanced, the particular saga of Trelleborg, or whatever it was called in those days, was never written down. Or if it was written down the manuscript is lost. We do not know their story and most likely we never shall.

WHO DISCOVERED AMERICA?

I CAN imagine someone in Mars, a few thousand years from now, saying 'Was it XYZ, or was it PQR, who discovered Earth?', and this sort of remark may be a little displeasing to the ordinary inhabitant of any of the five continents of the terrestrial globe (if any of them were left alive after a successful discovery from Mars). So when we say, 'Who discovered America?' it certainly shows us up. For there were whole nations already living in America with an elaborate culture of their own. The Inca civilisation in South America was far higher than that of their Spanish conquerors, and the North American Indians might, through time, have developed further. Their particular virtues and perceptions might have grown. Their vices might have changed. Who are we in Europe and White America today to say that we have done so much better than the American Indians might have done?

However, if we do ask this question, the answer is almost always 'Columbus', which only shows the importance of having a good Press. And, of course, it remains that Columbus and Amerigo Vespucci and their friends and colleagues had completely lost sight of the fact that there had ever been anyone before them. Large facts can drop out of history very easily if there is not somebody to report them and other people to see that the report is spread. Equally, something which is not a fact, but which powerful people would like us to believe, may rapidly come to be accepted. The first people to discover the continent of America were well reported in the sense that what they did and saw was vividly described. But the report was written in a language that most of Europe could not read – Icelandic – and was widely known only in the countries on the very fringe of Europe: Iceland and Greenland, and perhaps the other Norse lands. The much later report of Columbus was backed by an empire-building court and society who saw America as something potentially important and very valuable, something they must lay claim to. Whereas the Icelandic reports were merely a curiosity, even at the court of Denmark.

It is only lately that the reports of the earliest discoverers of America, the Vinland Sagas, have actually been known in the rest of Europe. Meanwhile thousands of history books have gone on repeating the Columbus story to millions of schoolchildren. And it is still not quite clear what happened in those early times. In fact I have not felt myself competent to judge between the versions. Some people even say that the Vinland Sagas are versions of an extremely good, realistic novel, but never in fact really happened. But I think there is enough evidence to confirm them and so do most historians, although I also like to think that there were such excellent novelists writing seven hundred years ago.

In the main, there are two stories of the discovery of America, one written in Greenland and the other in Iceland, and each one, naturally, showing a rather different point of view. It might easily have happened that one or other of these stories could have disappeared, for, of course, they are manuscripts, not printed books. One of them, dealing with events from the Greenland point of view, was written about 1380 by monks and is part of the Flatey Book, a long and splendid manuscript. By the courtesy of the Royal Library of Copenhagen I have myself been able to see and handle the Flatey Book. It is discoloured and sometimes torn, and the pages are of varying thickness. But the writing is black, even and legible, and occasionally someone of a later age has underlined or written in the margin. The capitals of the chapter headings are almost all beautifully decorated. When there are human figures they are the ordinary Gothic saints and grotesques, including a sinister little green mermaid being beheaded. But the animal figures are delicate and playful: the same queer little Iranian creatures that bite and twist their way anywhere between Ireland and China, and the decoration is done with exquisite delicacy in dark or bright red, or pale, vivid blue or green. Sometimes the tail of a letter will go right down the side of a page with cobweb-fine hanging lines. It made me think of miniature designs for the carving of the prow or the upper strake of a Viking ship. But the Flatey Book had its adventures. It belonged to John Torfasson, the farmer of Flatey, an island on the west of Iceland. In the mid-seventeenth century the Bishop of Iceland tried to buy it from him, first with money, then with land. Farmer John shook his head and refused to part with the family heirloom. But when the bishop was leaving the island the farmer came to see him off – and gave him the book. He sent it as a present to the King of Denmark; perhaps the safest thing that could happen to it, and that is how it is in Copenhagen today.

The other version, in Hauk's Book, had its adventures too. There were centuries during which such manuscripts were not valued and many of them were lost. Their pages might be used for binding sermons, or even for covering butter crocks. Many precious manuscripts may have been lost for ever that way, including the lost plays of Aeschylus and the lost poems of Sappho. Some of the northern ones might have told us still more about the people in the Vinland Sagas. But what luck that Hauk's Book and the Flatey Book are still with us!

It looks as though the first man actually to sight the American coast was an enterprising and courageous young man called Biarni. But he had also the caution that a good seaman usually has. His father was called Heriulf and was a neighbour and friend of Erik the Red; he decided to go and settle in Greenland with him and left Iceland probably in A D 986, while his son Biarni was trading over in Norway. Biarni came back to find his father had sailed and decided to follow him, though he knew it was dangerous 'seeing that none of us has ever been in the Greenland Sea'. Still, it was summer, and there was a fair easterly wind, so they kept their cargo on board, took in food and water and sailed.

But when they were out of sight of land the fair wind died and the north wind came up with fog, and they drifted for many days. I suppose they would keep a very careful look out, taking occasional soundings and listening for birds in case they were very near land without knowing. I remember myself coming in to the Shetland coast in fog, slowly, but, of course, knowing where we were, with an engine and compass and charts. We sounded our siren and at once the air was full of the near crying of birds and the fog slowly lifted and there was Noss Head, high and black above us. And if we had not known, if we had not had an engine to get away with –? In a fog, Biarni would not have dared to sail, and they would have no idea how they were going, for if the direction of the wind changed, so would their own direction, and they could never tell.

His merchant ship would have been a round ship, much beamier than the long-ships, with only enough oars to act as a very small auxiliary engine. It might have been partly decked, fore and aft, and the cargo from Norway, whatever it was – meal or corn, ship or house-building timber, wine or honey or other goods from farther south? – protected by hides stretched over it tarpaulin fashion. I think they must have been able to cook, although a good deal of their own provisions would have been meal which could be mixed cold with water, and ham. But I think they must have had a low wood-burning tripod with a flat stone under it; here they could roast meat or heat stones to drop into a pot for boiling. Nothing like this has been found, but of course anything of the kind would be taken out of a ship and might easily be broken up. There would be at least one dinghy, and, of course, plenty of bedding, the precious water-casks, and so on. It would have been a tiny floating world. Sometimes in the fog they might hear a whale blowing or turning over, perhaps see the interested black heads of seals peering at them from near by. And they must have fished. But it was a scaring time, most of all for Biarni, who had the responsibility.

At last the fog broke, and the sun came through, and they could see round them. There was no land. But at least they could tell direction by sun and stars. It was not as accurate a south as you would get with a watch, but still they were probably better at telling the time in their heads, even on a long summer day, than most of us are. They hoisted sail again and, after a day, or perhaps a day and night, they saw land. But where were they? They all talked about it as they sailed in closer, and all had some idea of what Greenland should look like, for they had been told about the ice mountains, and here were none to be seen.

In fact when they got nearer, they found this land was level and wooded, with only small hillocks on it. They decided it was not Greenland, but I think they must have come to the conclusion on the look of it that it was somewhere farther south, for they went about and sailed northward, leaving the land on their port bow. This shows that by the tenth century anyhow the sail must have been to some extent movable, though still nothing like the modern sail, mainly because the sheets, instead of being easy-running hemp ropes, were still hide thongs, or perhaps sometimes twisted out of cow-hair or horse-hair. I doubt if they could ever have sailed at all close to the wind, but obviously they could shove the yard round to some extent. But it must have been very hard work altering a course and hide thongs soaked with salt water must have been real agony on the hands for hauling.

Where were they? What they had done was to pass south of Cape Farewell, the southernmost point of Greenland, in the fog. Probably they passed far south, for by the time they had sailed three days from Iceland they would have got into the polar current, which perhaps was bringing the fog with it. This would have taken them south-west. Then, as it left them, and other main currents caught them, the southward drift might stop, and when the fog broke and they sailed they probably tried to sail due west or even north-west. But the Labrador current might have taken them south a bit. At any rate it is probable that the land they sighted was the Newfoundland coast, though some people say it was farther north.

They ran north along it for two days but getting out of sight of land, probably crossing White Bay, and sighting it again at Cape Bould or Southern Labrador. The crew asked Biarni what he thought, but again he was sure it was not Greenland for it was flat and wooded. Some of them wanted to land saying, particularly, that they needed wood and water. (The fact that they needed wood suggests that they did do some cooking.) But Biarni refused. Nobody knew what the landing might be like. It would be easy to lose ship, cargo and lives. Some of them were angry, but he was skipper and they had to agree. The wind was rising from the south-west and it was not safe to stay too near the coast. There might be islands or rocks and shoals, and it looks as though they were sailing both day and night. They needed plenty of sea room.

So they ran before south-westerly gales for three days and nights and then they saw a third land, high and mountainous, with ice on the mountains. This may have been Resolution Island on the north of the Hudson Straight. The crew asked Biarni if he would land here, but he said no 'because this land does not seem to me attractive'. So they never even lowered the sail but held their course off the land, and then realised that it was an island. Still the south-west gales held, growing stronger. Biarni told them to reef and keep a very careful eye on the sail and rigging. He would, of course, be at the steering oar. And so they held for another four days and nights, trying to keep an easterly course and not to be blown too far north. They may well have seen and felt in the air that they were getting too near the northern ice-fields.

At last they saw land again for the fourth time and asked Biarni what he thought about it. He answered that this really looked like Greenland,

Biarni, the skipper

and he would steer for it. So they did, and that evening they landed at a cape where they saw a boat, and it turned out to be the very cape where Biarni's father Heriulf lived, or so it says in the story. But of course it is also possible that they sailed near the coast, hailed a boat, and found out just where Heriulf's ness was! Anyhow, they made a safe landing, and no doubt Biarni disposed of his cargo even better than he could have done in Iceland. But naturally everyone asked him about the new land, and he found he had let himself in for a good deal of criticism, because he had done no exploring. The Greenlanders, who were finding life rather harder than perhaps even they had thought, were all excited about the possibility of a land with woods and level ground for farming. Why had Biarni not tried to see more of it? But Biarni seems to have had enough. He gave up voyaging and went to live with his father and farm Heriulfsness.

Heriulfsness became one of the most important places in Greenland. Brattahlid, where Erik the Red had settled, was always important, and later on there was to be a bishop's house with a small, strong cathedral built of huge stones and oak boards brought over from Norway. But we know about Heriulfsness in a queer way. Some thirty years ago a scientific expedition set out from Copenhagen and dug up the graves from the little churchyard there. Some of them were in frozen ground – in earth which had never been thawed since the graves were dug. And here they found the bodies in the clothes they had been buried in, the everyday woollen dresses and coats and hoods that the Greenlanders actually wore, men, women and children. And the people who were buried at Heriulfsness were probably the descendants of Biarni.

ERIK AND HIS NEIGHBOURS

WE come back to Erik the Red. He is not the kind of man to keep out of history. He and his friends and his children were not likely to settle down quietly to hard work and difficult house-keeping year after year, when there was a chance of something more exciting. He and his wife Thorhild had three sons, Leif, Thorvald, and Thorstein. They all seem to have been fine, intelligent and adventurous young men, and later on Leif was nicknamed 'The Lucky' because of his rescue of a shipwrecked crew; he was particularly longsighted. All the boys were probably born in Iceland before Erik and Thorhild came over to Greenland and settled at Brattahlid. He also had an illegitimate daughter, Freydis, who was intelligent and brave, but with a sense of grievance – she was married to a rather stupid and lowborn man for his money – which made her wickedly ambitious and ready to do anything to get her own ends.

Round Brattahlid there were plenty of friends and neighbours, the settlers who had come with Erik from Iceland, including Heriulf, Biarni's father. And on the Brattahlid steading there were several families besides Erik's own. There was a big, dark man, Thorhall the Hunter, who hunted and fished for Erik and helped him with the estate work. He was about Erik's age, a bad-tempered, overbearing kind of man, a worshipper of the god Thor and always trying to get the better of the Christians. There was also a nice little man with a worried look who was very fond of the boy Leif, in fact a kind of foster-father to him. He was called Tyrker and was a German, but whether he had been taken prisoner, brought north as a slave and then freed, or whether he just wandered north, we don't know. He may have been the kind that doesn't settle down when they are young, but by the time he got to Greenland he could not get any farther – until the chance came. Anyhow he was a clever little man and a good carpenter, just the sort that was needed in a colony. All that seems to me to be a fair deduction from the saga. I expect little Leif used to come and help him, stay all day long copying him, picking up shavings, helping him sharpen his tools, asking questions and listening to stories. When wood got scarce they probably went down to the beach together looking for driftwood – which had perhaps started with the trunk of a tree falling into the Hudson river – and pulling it in and observing the ways of the great sea.

Erik's three sons were just growing up when Biarni Heriulfsson came back from his voyage, and they were surely among the boys who teased Biarni for being so cautious. Doubtless they boasted of what they would have done themselves if they had sighted a new land! But there would be plenty else for them to do in Greenland, and as soon as Leif was old enough he set sail for Norway to visit the court of King Olaf Trygvasson. This would be part of his education and would feel much the same as it would for a young country squire, talking broad Dorset or Yorkshire, going to visit London Town a hundred and fifty years ago. But it was probably healthier. . .

On his way Leif was driven out of his course to the Hebrides, where he found plenty of other Norse people. He was held there most of the summer by contrary winds and fell in love with a well-born woman called Thorgunna, rather older than he was. She asked him to take her back with him, but he was frightened, as he thought her relations would be angry. In fact if he carried her off in his ship they might follow them and kill him. She told him she was going to have a child and she would bring him up – she was sure it was to be a boy – and send him over to Greenland. Leif gave her a gold ring, a heavy cloak of Greenland stuff and a belt of linked walrus ivory as love tokens, and then he sailed for Norway. But later on the child, who was a boy, came out to Greenland and Leif acknowledged him. There seems to be no reason why this story comes in at all, but if we had some of the lost books perhaps they would tell what happened to the boy Thorgils when he grew up.

Meanwhile Leif was well received by King Olaf, who thought him a very promising young man, and asked him to go and proclaim Christianity in Greenland. Leif himself accepted it quite easily and was baptised with all his crew. Probably one of the important men of the court, an earl or even the king himself, stood godfather to him. This meant that the godfather gave presents to the godson and looked after him to some extent. There is a story of one of the Norse toughs who was getting baptised and was given a new baptismal robe, but made of coarse cloth. He was very much put out and explained that whenever he had been baptised before he was always given a good white linen shirt, and he refused to be baptised again unless he got the same thing!

However, Leif brought back the king's message to Greenland and proclaimed Christianity. This was annoying for his father, old Red Erik, who did not hold with these newfangled religions, especially as his wife immediately took to it, changed her name from Thorhild to Thiodhild, built a church, and refused to sleep with him.

Meanwhile other people were coming out to Greenland. Vifil, the man who had been Aud's slave, and to whom she said after they got to Iceland that it did not matter whether or not he had land, for anyone could see he was noble, got his land and married, and his sons Thorgeir and Thorbiorn were fine men, well thought of, and they married into the families of the other settlers. Thorbiorn did particularly well. He had a very beautiful and intelligent daughter, called Thorid at first, though later when they changed over to Christianity her name too was changed, getting rid of Thor; now she was Gudrid. She spent a lot of her time with her foster-father Orm and his wife Halldis at a near-by farmstead. In the Norse countries, and in Iceland particularly, there was a great deal of fostering; it made for closer and friendlier relations, and knit the community together. If your friend fostered your child he was doubly your friend, you owed him protection. If you fostered your friend's child, you admitted that he was somewhat your superior, but you could appeal to him for help and advice.

But while Gudrid was staying with Orm and Halldis, she was courted by a rich, handsome, but rather showy young man, Einar, son of Thorgeir of Thorgeirsfells, a man who had been a slave, but who had been freed and become a very rich merchant. Einar was trading between Iceland and Norway, doing very well, and he gave presents to Orm and asked for his help in wooing the lovely Gudrid. Orm was doubtful about it, as he said Gudrid had already been asked in marriage; both she and her father were likely to be very particular about a husband for her.

But Einar pressed Orm to help him, saying he thought there was the chance of being accepted as he and his father were so rich in land and goods, while Gudrid's father Thorbiorn, though a most honourable man, was going downhill financially. Perhaps Thorbiorn was over-generous to his friends and liked to make too much of a show. Orm was still doubtful, but said he would see what he could do. So when Thorbiorn held an autumn feast for all his friends, Orm put forward Einar's proposal.

But Thorbiorn was furious and said he would never marry his daughter to the son of a thrall. This seems odd in someone who was himself the son of a thrall. There must have been more than that against Einar; perhaps Thorgeir, his father, was slave-minded as Vifil had never been. Yet it may well be that the generations have been telescoped in the telling and Aud's Vifil was really Thorbiorn's great-grand-father. But, at any rate, Thorbiorn felt himself deeply affronted, took Gudrid back from her foster-parents and the next spring held another feast, and said to his friends, who all, no doubt, would have heard about the refusal of Einar, that sooner than lose his honour by marrying Gudrid beneath her, he would give up his homestead and go out to Greenland to his old friend, Erik the Red.

Then he gave presents to all his friends, sold his lands and bought a ship. Thirty people joined him, among them Orm and Halldis, and they put out to sea in good weather. But once they were well out they ran into gales and lost their way and had a very miserable voyage. People fell sick, and half of them died, including Orm and Halldis, and they only got to Greenland just in time, on the very eve of winter.

They were all taken in very hospitably by a man called Thorkill, but it was a bad time in Greenland. The fishing had been poor, boats and men had been lost, and they were depending on the dried fish to carry them through until next year. Thorbiorn and Gudrid at least had been used to more comfort in Iceland, but it was better than storms and death at sea. Thorkill was the chief farmer in that part of the settlement, and everyone came to him for advice. They were all asking him how long the bad time would last. And he had a way of finding out, if he was pressed to use it, for there was a witch or prophetess in the settle-ment, one of nine witch sisters, and she could see into the future if all things were done rightly for her, as the custom was. Her name was Thorbiorg. Thorkill invited her to his home, and everyone would be there, including most of the guests from Iceland. But not Thorbiorn. He would not stay in the house and look on at their heathen rites; but young Gudrid was full of curiosity and excitement and half-fear; she stayed behind with the rest.

These were the short days of midwinter, but there would be a great fire after the few hours of daylight were over, and the house would be lighted with cruisies of seal-oil, and full of moving shadows and spaces of darkness.

'A high seat was prepared for the prophetess, in which a cushion filled with poultry feathers was placed. When she came in the evening with the man who had been sent to meet her, she was wearing a dark-blue coat, fastened with a strap, and set with stones quite down to the hem. She wore glass beads around her neck, and upon her head a black lamb-skin hood, lined with white cat-skin. In her hands she carried a staff, upon which there was a knob, which was ornamented with brass, and set with stones up about the knob. Circling her waist she wore a girdle of touchwood, and attached to it a great skin pouch, in which she kept the charms which she used when she was practising her sorcery. She wore upon her feet shaggy calf-skin shoes, with long, tough laces upon the ends of which there were large brass buttons. She had cat-skin gloves upon her hands, which were white inside and lined with fur. When she entered, all of the folk felt it to be their duty to offer her becoming greetings. She received the salutations of each individual according as he pleased her. Yeoman Thorkel took the sibyl by the hand and led her to the seat which had been made ready for her. Thorkel bade her run her eyes over man and beast and home. She had little to say concerning all these. The tables were brought out in the evening, and it remains to be told what manner of food was prepared.' They made her a beestie cheese from the first milking of a goat, and for her meat there were the hearts of every kind of beast, which could be obtained in Greenland.

'She had a brass spoon, and a knife with a handle of walrus tusk, with a double hasp of brass around the haft, and from this the point was broken. And when the tables were removed, Yeoman Thorkel approached Thorbiorg, and asked how she was pleased with the home, and the character of the folk, and how speedily she would be likely to become aware of that concerning which he had questioned her, and which the people were anxious to know. She replied that she could not give an opinion in this matter before the morrow, after she had slept there through the night. And on the morrow, when the day was far spent, such preparations were made as were necessary to enable her to accomplish her soothsaying. She bade them bring her those women, who

knew the incantation which she required to work her spells, and which
she called Warlocks. But such women were not to be found. On that a
search was made throughout the house, to see whether anyone knew
this incantation.'

And now young Gudrid became uneasy, for she knew that this was
something which she could do for her host, and yet she did not like to
do it. She must have wished her father were there to advise her, or perhaps that she had gone out with him. At last she felt she had to speak.
'Then says Gudrid: "Although I am neither skilled in the black art nor a
sibyl, yet my foster-mother, Halldis, taught me in Iceland that spell-song,
which she called Warlocks." Thorbiorg answered: " Then you are wise
in season." Gudrid replied: "This is an incantation and ceremony of
such a kind that I do not mean to lend it any aid, because I am a Christian woman." Thorbiorg answered: "The way it might be, you could
give your help to the company here, and still be no worse woman than
before; however, I leave it with Thorkel to provide for my needs."
Thorkel now so urged Gudrid, that she said she must needs do what he
wished her to do. The women then made a ring round about, while
Thorbiorg sat up on the spell-dais. Gudrid then sang the song, so sweet
and well, that no one remembered ever before to have heard the melody
sung with so fair a voice as this. The sorceress thanked her for the song,
and said: "She has indeed lured many spirits hither, who think it pleasant to hear this song, those who were wont to forsake us hitherto and
refuse to submit themselves to us. Many things are now revealed to me,
which hitherto have been hidden, both from me and from others. And
I am able to announce that this period of famine will not endure longer,
but the season will mend as spring approaches. The visitation of disease,
which has been so long upon you, will disappear sooner than was expected. And you, Gudrid, I shall reward out of hand, for the help
which you consented to give us, since the fate in store for you is now
all made plain to me. You will make a most worthy match here in
Greenland, but it will not last long, for your future path leads out to
Iceland and a great and goodly family of descendants shall come from
you. And above your line brighter rays of light shall shine, than I have
power clearly to unfold. And now fare well and health to you, my
daughter." After this the folk came up to the sibyl, and each one begged
for information concerning that about which he wanted to know most.
She was very ready in her answers, and little of that which she foretold
failed of fulfilment. After this they came for her from a neighbouring
farmstead, and thereupon set out thither.'

Then Thorbiorn came back and was told what had happened, but we do not know what he said about Gudrid, whether he was angry that she had taken part in heathen rites, or glad that she had done her duty as a guest. But at least the weather improved quickly, and spring opened well, just as Thorbiorg the white witch had prophesied.

'Thorbiorn equipped his ship and sailed away, until he arrived at Brattahlid. Erik received him with open arms, and said that it was well that he had come thither. Thorbiorn and his household remained with him during the winter, while quarters were provided for the crew among the farmers. And the following spring Erik gave Thorbiorn land on Stokkaness, where a goodly farmstead was founded, and there he lived thence-forward.'

So here were new neighbours for Erik the Red, and pleased enough he would be, and all the young men when they were not speaking about voyages of discovery would be sculling around to see if they could get a word with Gudrid, and word would have got about over the prophecy that there would be a worthy marriage in Greenland. And who would be thinking of the second part of the prophecy, the shortness of the first marriage and then the other marriage in Iceland? That might never come true, but this spring the golden-maned Gudrid was walking and singing in the sunshine under the young green feathers of birches and among the sweet scents of the ground willow and the delicate bright flowers of the Greenland May-time. The sons of Erik the Red would be watching her, and, most of all, Thorstein, the youngest boy.

LEIF AND HIS BROTHERS

At last all this talk about voyages of discovery began to turn into practical shape. It was about the year 1003, and Leif Eriksson, who was in his twenties, went to Biarni Heriulfsson and bought a ship from him and collected a crew, careful that they were the right sort. One of them was his old playmate, Tyrker, the German. At last he had another thirty-four men, and then he asked his father, Erik the Red, to be the leader of the expedition. But Erik's hair was more grey than red now. He did not think he would be able to stand up to the wear and tear of an exploring expedition.

But Leif tried to persuade him; he was a luck-bringer, the expedition would be no good without him. At last Erik said he would go. But on the way down to the ship the horse stumbled and threw him. He hurt his foot, or said he had hurt it, and decided not to go on, the omens were against it. But the rest sailed with Leif in command.

Leif was a big, powerful, imposing man, very wise and just for his years. There seems to be no doubt that he had the ability to lead the expedition. It looks as though they sailed almost due west and came to the land which Biarni saw last. They anchored near it and went ashore in the dinghy, but there was no grass, nothing but rocks and high mountains, and they could see no good in it. However, Leif said that at any rate they had done better than Biarni by landing and he would call it Helluland. This means the land of large flat stones, almost 'slateland'.

Then they put well out to sea again for safety's sake so as to get plenty of sea room, and sailed south, helped by the Labrador drift. When next they sighted land and went ashore, it was level and wooded, with broad stretches of white sand. This they called Markland (forest land), and no doubt they got water, and, if they needed it, wood. This was probably Labrador still, but may possibly have been Nova Scotia. Then they went out to sea again and sailed for two days and nights with the north-east wind until they sighted land again, and went ashore on an island in fine weather.

'They observed that there was dew upon the grass, and it so happened that they touched the dew with their hands, and touched their hands to their mouths, and it seemed to them that they had never before tasted anything so sweet as this. They went aboard their ship again and sailed into a certain sound, which lay between the island and a cape, which jutted out from the land on the north, and they stood in westering past the cape. At ebb-tide there were broad reaches of shallow water there, and they ran their ship aground there, and it was a long distance from the ship to the ocean; yet were they so anxious to go ashore that they could not wait until the tide should rise under their ship, but hurried to the land, where a certain river flows out from a lake. As soon as the tide rose beneath their ship, however, they took the boat and rowed to the ship, which they worked up the river, and so into the lake, where they cast anchor and carried their hammocks ashore from the ship, and built themselves huts there. Afterwards they made up their minds to establish themselves there for the winter, and accordingly they built a large house. There were plenty of salmon there both in the river or in the lake, and larger salmon than they had ever seen before. The country thereabouts seemed to be so good that cattle would need no fodder there during the winters. There was no frost there in the winters, and the grass only withered a little. The days and nights there were of more nearly equal length than in Greenland or Iceland.'

In fact it seemed just the kind of land which could well be colonised, and they began exploring systematically with this end in view. They divided up into two bands, of which one stayed at home while the other explored in all directions, but not so far that they would not get back the same evening. And the explorers in each of the bands were never to get separated from one another. Leif took turns with the explorers and the home party.

Where were they? I would expect it to be easy enough to say, but as a matter of fact it is extraordinarily difficult. A lot of people, both here and in Scandinavia and in America, have written books about it, all proving, to their authors' satisfaction, exactly where Leif Eriksson and the rest landed.

There is one very attractive theory put forward by Edward F. Gray in his book *Leif Eriksson, Discoverer of America*. According to him, they landed on Cape Cod, though neither he nor the others who believe in the Cape Cod theory are prepared to say just where, because the sandy coast here is constantly shifting, being eroded by currents or else re-made out of sandbanks. The Cape Cod peninsula had at one time – it is shown in the early American maps – an island called Nausit lying just off it, which has since been swept clean away. According to Gray they may have touched there first and then come in through Nantucket Sound to the island called Martha's Vineyard. This corresponds to the place where the ship ran aground and the lake they brought her into afterwards.

Yet this island may be bitterly cold in winter, not perhaps by Greenland's standards, but it would not be warm enough for cattle to be outwintered. However, there is an island only a few miles away which does not get nearly so cold, just because it is caught in the edge of the warm Gulf Stream current, and those who know about that part of the world say that a thousand years ago it might easily have been joined to Martha's Vineyard by a low tide sand strip since washed away. This island is called Noman's Land, and it has been suggested that the large house for winter was built there. Unfortunately this is not corroborated at all. There was a stone with a rather doubtful inscription on it in 'Runic'. But it could not have been put there by Leif. And, such as it was, it has now vanished. . . Nor were the excavators in 1940 able to find any evidence of Norse occupation.

It is rather a desolate island now, grassy and boggy, with low scrub, but in the peat there are large tree stumps and roots lying buried, and in an account of the island from the Gosnold Expedition of 1602 it was said to be overgrown with beech and cedar, as well as fruit bushes and vines. In those days there were plenty of deer and wild fowl. There are no deer now, and few wild fowl, but it is a great stopping place for the spring migrants in their long flight inland, and there are still plenty of berry bushes. I wonder whether it was the introduction of sheep to the island which killed out the trees, or at least stopped their natural regeneration from seedlings. The description of Noman's Land today reminds me of how some parts of Scotland have been ruined by sheep.

The other thing which suggests the Martha's Vineyard part of the world, is the name Straumey (Stream Isle) which occurs in one passage. This name might easily come from the strong currents which are constantly washing round and altering the shape of Martha's Vineyard. It also says of Straumey that at first there were so many birds there that it was scarcely possible to step between the eggs. This too might easily happen nowadays.

But there are many parts of the North American coasts where there are islands set among currents, and many sandy beaches. And I think it is certain that the climate has changed very much since the days of Leif Eriksson. Just as Greenland was less ice-covered then, so also the Canadian shores were less bleak and icy. Trees grew farther north. Vines must have grown farther north than they do now. The question is how far?

Some people say it all happened more than a thousand miles north, along the Labrador coast. Is it possible that the climate and perhaps the course of the Gulf Stream were so different, that vines might have grown there? Southern Labrador, after all, gets the same length of summer day as England, and supposing there was no ice-chilled water coming south along the coast on the Labrador drift, things might be very different. The Hamilton inlet on the Labrador coast has enough currents in it to be Streamfirth, and the fact that it is all very different now must not prejudice us too much.

Those who hold for the northern site say that it was quite impossible for Leif to have got as far south as Nantucket, on the evidence of his day's sailing. A certain amount depends on what you mean by a 'day'. But conditions may change again. If that is so, our grandchildren may yet see Labrador coming into its own. If the polar cold that steeps the toes of the cliffs were to relax, the coast might become beautiful, instead of barren and forbidding. The summer flowers are wonderful even now, azalea, gentian, berries of all kinds. Perhaps some day the grapes might come back. At any rate the coast might be systematically explored, as it has never been so far, by archaeologists looking for the traces which should be left of Leif's house.

But I am almost sure that Gray is right about one thing. He suggests that one or two passages out of the story of the later explorer, Thorfinn Karlsefni, should really belong to Leif's first voyage. There is, for instance, a very peculiar one about the two 'Gaels' given to Leif by King Olaf, the man called Haki and the woman Haekia. In the story they

Happy Tyrker

were swifter than deer and dressed in a kind of long plaid open at the sides. They were put ashore and told to run. On the third day they came back, one with a bunch of grapes (not necessarily ripe), and the other with an ear of self-sown wheat. It is a nice story, but my feeling is that it is all too like a fairy-tale; their names are fairy-tale names and they do things which might be verses in a song.

However, there is one other adventure which is very real. 'It was discovered one evening that one of their company was missing, and this proved to be Tyrker, the German. Leif was very much upset by this, for Tyrker had lived with Leif and his father for a long time, and had been particularly devoted to Leif, when he was a child. Leif was extremely angry with his companions, and prepared to go in search of him, taking twelve men with him. They had only gone a short distance from the house, when they were met by Tyrker and they received him most cordially. Leif saw at once that his foster-father was in lively spirits. Tyrker had a prominent forehead, restless eyes and small features; he was short and rather a sorry-looking individual, but for all that, he was a most capable handicraftsman. Leif spoke to him, asking, "What kept you so late, my own foster-father, and why did you stray from the others?" To begin with Tyrker talked for some time in German, rolling his eyes, and grinning, and they could not understand him; but after a time he spoke to them in the northern tongue: "I did not go much farther than you, and yet I have something new to tell you. I have found vines and grapes." "Is this really true, foster-father?" said Leif. "Most certainly it is true," said he, "for I was born where there are plenty of grapes and vines."'

I think this must have meant that the ingenious Tyrker had been collecting the grapes and letting them ferment. He had remembered how it had been done at home, in south Germany perhaps. But it was good enough. Probably the Greenlanders had all eaten imported dried grapes, raisins – think how delicious they would be in a community with little fruit and no sugar! – and they knew what a valuable cargo they could get. This must have happened in late autumn, after they had finished their winter house, and while they were exploring. 'They slept the night through, and the next day Leif said to his shipmates: "We will now divide our labour, so as to get a cargo of these for my ship." They acted on this advice, and it is said that their after-boat was filled with grapes. A cargo sufficient for the ship was cut, and when the spring came, they made their ship ready, and sailed away; and from its products Leif gave the land a name, and called it Vinland.'

The vines would probably have been used for shipbuilding instead of the willow withies which were often used to lash together the planks and knees of the boats and to make the rowing benches fast to the ribs; and, of course, good timber had all to be imported into Greenland, so it was very valuable. The grapes would have been dried in the rays of the sun, or even inside the house on hot stones or metal. I expect their cattle were in decent condition too after a better wintering than they had ever had in Greenland.

In spring they loaded cargo and cattle, and many of them, I expect, intended to come back. Among the wood was some that they called Masur. It was thought very highly of, and some people say it was maple: the same which made 'maser' bowls in the late Middle Ages. But maple may be a secondary meaning. It may really have been well figured wood of any kind, or even particularly useful wood such as the wind-twisted oaks of the American coast which would be wonderful for shipbuilding, as they are ready shaped for knees and ribs.

They had fair winds as far as Greenland, and here they rescued fifteen people from a skerry where they had been wrecked, using their second little dinghy, as the big one was filled with dried grapes. In one story the rescued people seemed to have included Gudrid and a husband called Thori who later died. But I cannot help wondering if it was not a different Gudrid. Now Leif came back with a very valuable cargo and much honour and glory. His father died that winter, and he inherited Brattahlid and settled down there. It would have taken him all his time to farm the property.

But his next brother Thorvald wanted to go back and explore farther, and perhaps bring home another rich cargo. Leif said he might have the ship, but first he must go and fetch the wood that was still left on the skerry where the wrecked ship had gone ashore. This shows how very valuable wood was in Greenland.

So the next year Thorvald set out with thirty men. All seems to have gone well, and they duly found Leif's huts still standing and laid up the ship. I am sure some of Thorvald's crew must have been on Leif's voyage. One man whom they seem to have taken from Brattahlid was Thorhall the hunter. They spent a quiet winter and then went exploring along the coast among fields and islands and woods. 'They found neither dwelling of man nor lair of beast; but in one of the westerly islands, they found a wooden building for the shelter of grain. They found no other trace of human handiwork, and they turned back, and arrived at Leif's huts in the autumn.'

Gray thinks that the story of Thorhall the hunter really belongs here, and this is what happened one time when they were short of food: 'Thorhall the hunter disappeared. They had already prayed to God for food, but it did not come as promptly as their necessities seemed to demand. They searched for Thorhall for three half-days, and found him on a projecting crag. He was lying there, and looking up at the sky, with mouth and nostrils gaping, and mumbling something. They asked him why he had gone there; he answered, that this was nobody else's business. They asked him then to go home with them, and he did so. Soon after this a whale appeared there, and they captured it, and flensed it, and no one could tell what sort of whale it was; and when the cooks had prepared it, they ate it, and were all made ill by it. Then Thorhall, approaching them, says: "Did not the Red-Beard prove more helpful than your Christ? This is my reward for the verses which I composed to Thor the Trustworthy; seldom has he failed me." When the people heard this, they threw the whale back into the sea, and made their appeals to God. The weather then improved, and they could now row out to fish, and thenceforward they had no lack of provisions, for they could hunt game on the land, gather eggs on the island, and catch fish from the sea.'

In another story he comes out as a grumbler and unpopular. It looks as though he came to some kind of bad end, possibly in Ireland, and it seems as though he took the larger of their boats with him and lost it. Anyhow he made a wonderful opportunity for propaganda against heathen practices by the saga-writers!

The second summer they set out in the other direction north-east, and there they had something of a disaster. They were driven ashore and damaged their keel. They had, I think, to beach the ship and cut timber for a new keel – no joke to get a straight tree long enough and preferably oak. There probably were oaks, but it would be hard to find one near the coast which was not windblown and twisted. It would all have to be axe cut into shape and the whole thing would take time and a lot of trouble, but they managed it. Then they dug a hole in the sand, stood the old keel up in it and called the place Keelness. After that they sailed round a point and down into a bay, which seems to have been sheltered, well wooded and beautiful; here they all went ashore, Thorvald saying that it was here he would like to make his home. But when they went back to the ship they found on the sands the thing which so far nobody had seen – the original inhabitants; three men hiding under each of three skin canoes. The Greenlanders seized and killed all the men but one. He escaped, and it was the worse for them, because this one man who got away was able to tell his friends of the danger.

But it was a warm day. Thorvald and his men had walked and fought and killed, and probably eaten and drank. 'They were then so over-powered with sleep that they could not keep awake, and all fell into a heavy slumber, from which they were awakened by the sound of a cry uttered above them, and the words of the cry were these: "Awake, Thorvald, you and all your company, if you would save your life; and board your ship with all your men, and sail with all speed from the land!" A countless number of skin-canoes then advanced toward them from the inner part of the firth, whereupon Thorvald exclaimed: "We must put out the war-boards, on both sides of the ship, and defend our-selves as well as we can, but offer little attack." This they did, and the Skraelings, after they had shot at them for a time, fled precipitately, each as best he could. Thorvald then asked his men, whether any of them had been wounded, and they told him that no one of them had received a wound. "I have been wounded in my armpit," says he; "an arrow flew in between the gunwhale and the shield, below my arm. Here is the shaft, and it will bring me to my end. I counsel you now to retrace your way with the utmost speed. But you shall carry me to that headland which seemed to me to offer so pleasant a dwelling-place; in this way it may be fulfilled, that the truth sprang to my lips, when I wished I might stay there for a time. You shall bury me there, and place a cross at my head, and another at my feet, and call it Crossness for ever after."'

I think here the man who wrote the story is trying to make out that they were warned by a heavenly voice, and links it up with the Cross. I am quite sure the monks who set it all down felt it was their duty to put in that sort of moral whenever they could.

In another version of the story it is a 'uniped', that is a creature with one foot, who shoots Thorvald. Here Thorvald 'was sitting at the helm, and the uniped shot an arrow into his inwards. Thorvald drew out the arrow, and exclaimed: "There is fat around my paunch; we have hit upon a fruitful country, and yet we are not like to get much profit of it." Thorvald died soon after from this wound. Then the uni-ped ran away back toward the north.'

This then is the first mention of the original inhabitants of America, the Skraelings. But – who were the Skraelings?

We cannot be quite sure who were the ordinary inhabitants of Vin-land, wherever it may have been, at this particular part of history. But we can at least be sure they had two feet. The unipeds were probably put in by some monk, who was writing out the story and felt the need of a classical atmosphere, for unipeds come straight out of Herodotus. There were Red Indians in the interior of America at this time, but they in their turn had probably not yet conquered the shores and islands which were still used for hunting and gathering grounds by a scattered people akin to the Eskimos, probably not cultivators of the soil and using only stone weapons. But the descriptions of them, as we shall see, are not very accurate, though it does sometimes seem as if two different kinds of people had been seen. To the Greenlanders the Skraelings were merely a natural obstacle not interesting in themselves.

So there was Thorvald dead and buried on a far foreign strand, the first white man's grave in America. And that was the news they had to take back to his brothers, Leif and Thorstein, when the next spring they sailed again to Greenland, and brought their cargo of dried grapes and timber safe to Brattahlid.

Thorstein had married Gudrid in spite of the prophecy, but that did not stop him from going to find and bring back his brother's body. He meant to go straight to Crossness and back, not stopping for a cargo. So he put food and water aboard the same ship, took a crew of twenty-five, including surely some who had been with Thorvald, and with them his young wife Gudrid. And so they sailed. But they had bad luck with the weather; all through that summer they were blown about hither and thither and lost all reckoning. Thorstein was probably not a very experienced sailor. Nobody knows what Gudrid thought. But the end of it was they were driven back to Greenland worn out with the struggle they had been having, and Thorvald's body still in America.

THE MAN WITH THE
MAKINGS OF A HERO

THERE was Biorn Ironside, son of Ragnar Lodbrok, who went harrying in the Mediterranean in the early days of the opening out of the Swan's Road. Seven generations on from him and we come to Thorfinn, son of Thord Horsehead, who was nicknamed Karlsefni – 'man-promise' or 'with the makings of a hero'. By another side he was descended from Irish kings. And now he was a successful trader living in Iceland, with a ship of his own. In summer of the year 1009 Thorfinn Karlsefni fitted out this ship and took a cargo, mostly of food and household stuffs, for the Greenland market. He might have had some livestock, cows or sheep, or even a horse or two; these would have been the lovely pale-coloured Iceland ponies with the dark stripe down the back which shows up so well on a hogged mane. A fair-haired man in a red cloak, with gold on arms and neck, riding one of these would have looked very well indeed.

One of his friends, Snorri Thorbrandson, went with him. Meanwhile two other friends of his, Icelanders too, Biarni Grimolfsson and Thorhall, decided to do the same thing; their ship was about the same size as his, and they sailed together. Both ships put into Eriksfirth in the autumn, and Leif and the rest rode down to the ships. There was a good trade, and among the women who were turning over the household

THE MAN WITH THE MAKINGS OF A HERO

goods and dress stuffs was Gudrid. Thorfinn Karlsefni said to her that she should take whatever of his goods she wanted.

It was about a year now since Gudrid had landed after Thorstein's disastrous voyage to look for his brother's body. And they had come back to a winter of sickness. There are two stories about what happened and both of them are dark and twisty. But it seems to have been something like this. Thorstein and Gudrid were staying with another couple: Thorstein the Dark and his wife Grimhild. They had not taken to Christianity and he was supposed to be a difficult kind of man, but he was very kind to the young couple. Gudrid was a clever, friendly girl, and had no trouble fitting in with strangers. There would be just the one main room at the farmstead, with beds curtained off round it. They all crowded in. Winter came on and some kind of sickness with it. The men who had been on Thorstein's ship had little resistance left, and thus many of them died. Then Thorstein, Gudrid's husband, got ill himself, and so did Grimhild, the housewife, a big, strong woman. At the height of her illness she needed to go to the privy by the outer door of the house, and Gudrid was helping her. Suddenly she cried out, and Gudrid blamed herself, thinking the older woman was catching a chill. But Grimhild had been caught by the Sight, as happens to people sometimes in the Highlands. She saw all the dead, including Thorstein Eriksson, Gudrid's husband, and at last herself. But with the terror of seeing her own fetch, the thing passed, and she let Gudrid help her back, and then she lay down to die. After that her husband, Thorstein the Dark, went out to get coffin boards, and Thorstein Eriksson cried out in the nightmare of his last fever that the dead woman was moving, was feeling for her shoes under the bed, was coming up to him!

But Thorstein the Dark came in and the body of his wife, Grimhild, was truly dead, and he put it into the coffin, and took it out. Then Thorstein Eriksson died, and Gudrid was grieving and crying, sitting on a stool by her young husband's body, which Thorstein the Dark had taken out of the bed and laid on a bench. It was the middle of the long, dark night, the small flame of the cruisies flickering, bitter cold outside, and a grinding and knocking of ice from off the sea. Thorstein the Dark picked up Gudrid in his arms and kissed her and petted her and promised to take her back to Eriksfirth with the body of young Thorstein, and do anything at all to help her. And he would find another woman to stay in the house with her. So at last she stopped crying and thanked him.

And then the body of her husband sat up and spoke, saying 'Where

is Gudrid?' Three times over it said this, and she was too frightened to
answer. Then Thorstein the Dark carried her over and, while she sat on
his knee, with his arms round her, he answered 'What do you wish,
namesake of mine?' Then the body of Thorstein Eriksson answered,
telling Gudrid, his widow, that there was a great future before her.
She would marry an Icelander and have a long wedded life and noble
children, but in the end she would outlive her husband and travel to
the south but come back and raise a church and take the Veil before her
own death. And after that the body stopped speaking and became truly
dead.

Thorstein the Dark was true to all the promises he had made to
Gudrid, and took her and her husband's frozen body back to Eriksfirth
in the spring, and after a time he settled there himself, and he was
thought well of by everyone. And Leif looked after his young sister-
in-law and thought that surely she was a good match, and he must see
that she married again when the right man came for her. She was thin
and pale at the end of that winter, but as summer came on she got back
her colour and began to sing again.

Leif asked Thorfinn and his crew, as well as Biarni and Thorhall and
their crew, to stay with them over winter at Brattahlid. Whatever had
not yet been sold was put into store there, and they all kept Christmas
together with great cheeriness and a feast, helped out by stores from
the ships, which held not only meal and corn, but malt for brewing.
And after the feast Thorfinn Karlsefni asked for Gudrid's hand in marriage, and so it was arranged, and it was thought in Greenland that this
way Gudrid was most likely to fulfil the destiny that had been laid on
her years before by the prophetess.

But the men were for ever talking about Vinland, and the great things
yet to be done there, and Leif would show Karlsefni the masur wood
and vines that he had brought back, and probably furs and feathers and
dried fruits or seeds, and queer stones. And he would tell over all the
landmarks and talk about currents and shoals and what were the likeliest
winds. Karlsefni asked Gudrid what she wanted, and Gudrid said she
would like to go and settle there, which shows that she herself did not
take the Iceland part of the prophecy too seriously. So it was decided,
and sixty men, five of them married with young wives who were willing to take the risk, agreed to come with them. The agreement was
that they should all share equally in any profits they made. Biarni
Grimolfsson decided to come with them and fitted out his ship too.
They took with them not only provisions and weapons, but all kinds

of settlers' goods, cows and a bull, sheep and a ram, poultry and so on, and Leif said he would lend them his house on the island off the coast of Vinland. So when summer came on they sailed.

Little is said about the voyage, but I think one gets the feel of it in Kipling's *The Finest Story in the World*. They seem to have followed Leif's own first course and not to have tried to sail straight across to Vinland. And Biarni Grimolfsson lost his ship, which must have been an old one, or not well enough tarred to keep off the boring worms which eat through wood. This is the story:

'Biarni, Grimolf's son, and his companions were driven out into the Atlantic, and came into a sea, which was filled with worms, and their ship began to sink under them. They had a boat, which had been coated with seal-tar; this the sea-worm does not penetrate. They took their places in this boat, and then found out that it would not hold them all. Then said Biarni: "Since the boat will not hold more than half of our men, it is my advice, that the men who are to go in the boat be chosen by lot, for a choice like this must not be made according to rank." This seemed to them all such a manly offer that no one opposed it. So they adopted his plan, the men casting lots; and it fell to Biarni to go in the boat, and half of the men with him, for it would not hold more. But when the men were come into the boat, a young Icelander, who was in the ship, and who had accompanied Biarni from Iceland, said: "Are you truly meaning, Biarni, to forsake me here?" "It must be even so," answers Biarni. "That was never the promise you gave my father," he answers, "when I left Iceland with you: to leave me behind like this, when you promised him that it should always be the same for both of us!" "So be it, it shall be changed thus," answers Biarni: "do you come here, and I will go to the ship, for I see well how eager you are for life." Biarni thereupon boarded the ship, and this man entered the boat, and they went their way, until they came to Dublin in Ireland, and there they told this tale. Now it is the belief of most people, that Biarni and his companions perished in the maggot-sea, for they were never heard of afterward.'

Karlsefni and his crew seem to have found Leif's Helluland with the great bare stones and the Arctic foxes. Farther south they came to his forest land, and also an islet with a bear on it, which they called Bear Island. Then they sailed south and came to the keel of Thorvald's ship still standing alone on Keelness. Here they found long, sandy beaches which they called Furdustrandir (the wonder beaches, as in the old fairy-tale). There are no long beaches like that in Iceland or Norway, and the old name would have been hanging in their heads. If it was Cape Cod where they were, and the northern point of it Keelness, as some people think, then it may be that they saw the strange mirage effects that people still see there. But there is a long sandy beach in Labrador too, and, though now it is bitter cold, it might have been different then.

Afterwards they found Straumfiord, with the currents and shoals that Leif had told them about, and finally they found his huts still standing on the island of currents and went ashore very thankfully with their beasts and bedding. Here they had a bit of luck, for a whale came ashore and they killed and flensed it, and they had any amount of whale-steak to eat along with the grapes and berries and nuts and game and all the good things that they could gather.

The cattle were turned out to graze and got very wild. Karlsefni had trees felled and split to season, and some of the men went out on exploring parties, sometimes for some distance into the interior of the country. It seemed to them unusually rich. 'They found self-sown wheat-fields on the land there, wherever there were hollows, and wherever there was hilly ground, there were vines. Every brook there was full of fish. They dug pits on the shore where the tide rose highest and when the tide fell, there were halibut in the pits. There were great numbers of wild animals of all kinds in the woods. They remained there half a month, and enjoyed themselves, and kept no watch.'

Meanwhile Gudrid gave birth to a boy, the first white baby to be born in America. But the next thing that happened was that the Skraelings came. There are two versions, one from the Flatey Book and one from Hauk's Book, and it is not quite clear exactly what did happen. It looks as though one encounter had been while Karlsefni and Snorri were exploring. 'One morning early, when they looked about them, they saw a great number of skin-canoes, and staves were brandished from the boats, with a noise like flails, and they were revolved in the same direction in which the sun moves. Then said Karlsefni: "What can this mean?" Snorri, Thorbrand's son, answers him: "It may be, that this is a signal of peace, so let us take a white shield and hold it up." And thus they did. Thereupon the strangers rowed toward them, and went upon the land, marvelling at those whom they saw before them. They were swarthy men, and nasty-looking, and the hair of their heads was ugly; they had great eyes, and were broad of cheek. They stayed there for a time looking curiously at the people they saw before them, and then rowed away, and to the southward around the point.'

The staves brandished from the boats were obviously double canoe paddles. I wonder why the explorers thought the Skraelings would recognise the white shield as a sign of peace? Perhaps in the early months there had been rather more dealings with them than it says in the story. For the next time they came they had furs to barter. One morning in spring it says they saw 'a great number of skin-canoes, rowing from the south past the cape, so numerous that it looked as if coals had been scattered broadcast out across the bay; and on every boat staves were waved. Thereupon Karlsefni and his people put out their shields, and when they came together, they began to barter with each other. Especially did the strangers wish to buy red cloth, for which they offered in exchange furs and all-grey skins. They also wanted to buy swords and spears, but Karlsefni and Snorri forbade this, just as later traders refused at first to sell guns to the "natives". In exchange for perfect clean skins, the Skraelings would take red stuff a span in length, which they would bind around their heads. So their trade went on for a time, until Karlsefni and his people began to grow short of cloth, when they divided it into such narrow pieces, that it was not more than a finger's breadth wide, but the Skraelings still continued to give just as much for this as before, or more.

'It so happened, that a bull, which belonged to Karlsefni and his people, ran out from the woods, bellowing loudly. This so terrified the Skraelings, that they rushed out to their canoes, and then rowed away to the southward along the coast. For three entire weeks nothing more was seen of them.'

The other version adds that 'Karlsefni had the women carry out milk to the Skraelings, which they no sooner saw, than they wanted to buy it, and nothing else. Now the outcome of the Skraelings' trading was, that they carried their wares away in their stomachs, while they left their packs and furs behind with Karlsefni and his companions, and having made this exchange they went away.'

Karlsefni had a strong wooden palisade set up round the house, as was done by settlers in Indian country seven hundred years later. And in the house within the stockade Gudrid looked after little Snorri, the baby.

There was another visit from trading Skraelings bringing the same grey squirrel and sable pelts. There is a story of Gudrid sitting inside the house beside the baby's cradle when a Skraeling woman dressed in black with a fillet round her head came in at the door. 'Her hair was of a light chestnut colour, and she was pale of hue, and so big-eyed, that never

6

before had eyes so large been seen in a human skull.' The story says that she and Gudrid talked to one another, and then the woman vanished. Perhaps Gudrid was scared and began imagining things.

But after this there was no more peaceful trading. Perhaps the Skraelings thought it was time to get rid of the white men, and perhaps they were right. It is not really very clear whether this was the first or second summer after they came. But anyhow, 'a great multitude of Skraeling boats was discovered approaching from the south, as if a stream were pouring down, and all of their staves were waved in a direction contrary to the course of the sun, and the Skraelings were all uttering loud cries. Thereupon Karlsefni and his men took red shields and displayed them.' This is rather puzzling. But it seems at any rate as if the Skraelings were yelling war-cries.

Then 'the Skraelings sprang from their boats, and they met them, and fought together. There was a fierce shower of missiles, for the Skraelings had war-slings. Karlsefni and Snorri observed, that the Skraelings raised upon a pole a great ball-shaped body, almost the size of a sheep's belly, and nearly black in colour, and this they hurled from the pole up on the land above Karlsefni's followers, and it made a frightful noise, where it fell. At that a great fear seized upon Karlsefni and all his men, so that they could think of nothing but flight, and of making their escape up along the river bank; for it seemed to them, that the troop of the Skraelings was rushing towards them from every side, and they did not pause until they came to a certain jutting crag, where they offered a stout resistance.'

There is then a story of one of the women running out, picking up the sword of one of the Icelanders who had been killed and frightening the Skraelings with it. After that the men all picked themselves up, found that two of their number had been killed and a great number of Skraelings. They bound up their wounds, went home and talked about the queer panic that had got at them.

The other version, in the Flatey Book, says nothing about the panic nor even that any Icelander or Greenlander was killed. In addition 'the Skraelings advanced to the spot which Karlsefni had selected for the encounter, and a battle was fought there, in which great numbers of the band of the Skraelings were slain. There was one man among the Skraelings, of large size and fine bearing, whom Karlsefni concluded must be their chief. One of the Skraelings picked up an axe, and having looked at it for a time, he brandished it around one of his companions, and hewed at him, and on the instant the man fell dead. Thereupon the big man seized the axe, and after examining it for a moment, he hurled it as far as he could, out into the sea; then they fled helter-skelter into the woods.'

Perhaps there were several battles of Indians, and one would be remembered and handed down in one family, and one in another. The axe story also appears like this. 'The Skraelings, moreover, found a dead man, and an axe lay beside him. One of their number picked up the axe, and struck at a tree with it, and one after another they tested it, and it seemed to them to be a treasure, and to cut well; then one of their number seized it, and hewed at a stone with it, so that the axe broke, whereat they concluded that it could be of no use, since it would not withstand stone, and they cast it away.'

There seems to have been another exploring expedition. 'They sailed to the northward off the coast, and found five Skraelings, dressed in skin-coats, lying asleep near the sea. There were vessels beside them, containing animal marrow mixed with blood. Karlsefni and his company concluded that they must have been banished from their own land. They put them to death. They afterwards found a cape, upon which there was a great number of animals, and this cape looked as if it were one cake of dung, by reason of the animals which lay there at night.' You will notice that Karlsefni decided that the sleeping Skraelings were outlaws, and that he could kill them with a good conscience! I expect he took their furs.

By now they had been in Vinland for two and a half years, three good mild winters when the beasts could graze all the time and two hot summers. People were beginning to quarrel, wanting to take one anothers' wives. It was obviously unpractical to try to start a colony with so few women. I expect there were some other babies born besides little Snorri, but the story does not say. They decided to go home, and no doubt by this time they had a wonderful cargo. Perhaps they left behind some of the sheep and cattle for the next people who might come. They sailed with the southerly wind, and put in at Markland, 'where they found five Skraelings, of whom one was bearded, two were women, and two were children. Karlsefni and his people took the boys, but the others escaped, and these Skraelings sank down into the earth. They carried the lads off with them, and taught them to speak, and they were baptized. They said that their mother's name was Vaetilldi, and their father's Uvaegi. They said that kings governed the Skraelings, one of whom was called Avalldamon, and the other Valldidida.

'They stated that there were no houses there, and that the people

lived in caves or holes. They said that there was a land on the other side
next their own country which was inhabited by people who wore
white garments, and yelled loudly, and carried poles before them, to
which rags were attached; and people believe that this must have been
Hvitramanna-land (White-men's-land) or Ireland the Great.' That is to
say, the country of complete myth was pushed back a little to the
'other side' of the Skraelings' country. One wonders what the poor
little Skraelings were trying to say. Nansen suggests that they are really
fairy-tale names, though another commentator thinks they might have
been Eskimo sentences, misunderstood. But Nansen seems to feel fairly
certain that there is a great deal of fairy-tale stuff in all the Vinland
stories. His comments are always extremely interesting, and his big
book *In Northern Mists*, takes you down all kinds of fascinating by-
ways.

There was one other Vinland voyage, this time again with two ships.
One of them was commanded by two Icelanders, brothers who had
been spending the winter in Greenland, Helgi and Finnbogi. The other
belonged to Freydis, the daughter of Erik the Red, who had inherited
his courage and toughness, but not his sense of honour and loyalty, and
her rather characterless husband, Thorvald. The two parties agreed to
share everything as the others had done, and Leif agreed to lend his
house again. I expect Leif must often have wanted to go back to Vinland himself, but since his father's death he would have had his hands
full, looking after things at Brattahlid. Freydis and the brothers had
agreed too that each should take thirty able-bodied men, besides the
women, but Freydis hid another five on board her ship, and this was
not discovered by the brothers until after they landed.

The brothers' ship got there a little sooner than the other – it was a
bigger ship – and Helgi and Finnbogi had their baggage carried up to
the house. 'Now when Freydis arrived, her ship was discharged, and
the baggage carried up to the house. Then Freydis exclaimed: "Why
did you carry your baggage in here?" "Because we believed," said
they, "that all the promises made to us would be kept." "It was to me
that Leif lent the house," said she, "and not to you." On that Helgi exclaimed: "We brothers can never hope to be as dishonest as you!" So
they carried their baggage out, and built a hut, above the sea, on the bank
of the lake, and put all in order about it. Meanwhile Freydis ordered
wood to be felled, to load up her ship with. The winter now set in,
and the brothers suggested that they should amuse themselves by

playing games. This they did for a time, until the folk began to disagree, and quarrels sprang up between them. Then the games came to an end, and the visits between the houses ceased; and it went on like this far into the winter.

One morning early, Freydis got up from her bed, and dressed herself, but did not put on her shoes and stockings. A heavy dew had fallen, and she took her husband's cloak, and wrapped it about her, and then walked to the brothers' house, and up to the door which had been only partly closed by one of the men, who had gone out a short time before. She pushed the door open, and stood, silently, in the doorway for a time. Finnbogi, who was lying on the inner side of the room, was awake, and said: "What do you want here, Freydis?" She answered, "I want you to get up, and go out with me, for I have something to say to you." He did so, and they walked to a tree which lay close by the wall of the house, and sat down upon it. "How do you like it here?" said she. He answered: "I am well pleased with this fertile land, but I am not at all pleased at the quarrel which has separated us, for it seems to me there has been no cause for it." "It is exactly as you say," she answered, "and I quite agree: this is why I am here to see you: I want to exchange ships with you brothers because you have a larger ship than mine, and I want to go away." "I suppose I have got to agree to this," he said, "if it is what you want." On that they separated and she returned home, and Finnbogi to his bed. She climbed up into bed, and woke Thorvald up with her cold feet, and he asked her why she was so cold and wet. She answered, in a furious temper, "I have been to the brothers," says she, "to try to buy their ship, for I wanted to have a bigger one, but they took what I suggested so badly that they struck me, and knocked me about very roughly; and all this time you, you poor wretch, will neither avenge my shame nor your own! And I find, of course, that I am no longer in Greenland! Anyhow I shall leave you unless you take vengeance for this." And now he could stand her taunts no longer, and ordered the men to get up at once, and take their weapons.

This they did, and went straight over to the house of the brothers, and entered it, while the folk were asleep, and seized and bound them, and led each one out, when he was bound. And as they came out, Freydis had each one killed. This way all of the men were put to death and only the women were left, and nobody would kill them. At this Freydis shouted out: "Hand me an axe!" This was done, and she fell on the five women and left them dead. They went home after this dreadful business, and it was perfectly clear that Freydis was delighted with what she had done. She spoke to her companions, saying: "If it is our fate to come again to Greenland, I will see to it that whoever speaks of what has happened shall die. We must give it out, that we left them living here, when we came away." Early in the spring, they equipped the ship, which had belonged to the brothers, and freighted it with all the products of the land, whatever they could get hold of and which the ship would carry. Then they put out to sea, and after a prosperous voyage, arrived with their ship in Eriksfirth early in the summer.'

No doubt Freydis and her husband said the brothers would be following them. They found Karlsefni at home, with his ship ready to sail for Norway, and loaded with goods from Vinland, furs, raisins, vines and so on. 'People say that a ship richer laden than that which he commanded never left Greenland.' He sailed without finding out what had happened.

Freydis went back home and hoped to bribe all her crew to silence. But stories began to go round sooner or later, for this kind of thing never pays in the long run. At last the rumours got to Leif, and he was terribly upset. He got hold of three of her crew and forced the story out of them. "'I have no heart," says Leif, "to punish my sister, Freydis, as she deserves, but this I predict of them, that there is little prosperity in store for their family." Hence it came to pass that no one from that time forward thought them worthy of anything but evil.' Perhaps they were outlawed, or perhaps merely boycotted, which would have been bad enough in a small community. At least they did not get away with it. But nobody else would ever want to go back to Leif's house, nor try to colonise a land which had been so hideously blood-stained.

But Karlsefni and Gudrid and little Snorri got safely to Norway. He sold his cargo very well, and he and Gudrid were asked out everywhere and enjoyed themselves very much, and no doubt both of them told the most exciting stories of their adventures. After he had sold everything else, a man from Bremen came and offered him half a gold mark for some kind of ornament – perhaps a weather vane – which was made out of masur wood from Vinland. After that they sailed back to Iceland and bought an estate, and everything went well with them. They had killed the dragon and taken his treasure just as their forefathers had done. And in the end all that had been prophesied about Gudrid in the dark Greenland night was fulfilled. After Karlsefni's death she went on a pilgrimage to Rome and made the round of the holy places there, and doubtless had an interview with the Pope himself, and came back to Iceland and became a nun, which was another very honourable thing to do. And from her and Karlsefni were descended many fine and honourable men and women, poets, bishops, adventurers and farmers with the wives and mothers whose courage and intelligence and generosity helped them to make a civilisation.

EPILOGUE

THIS, then, gives you an idea of the way these Norse people travelled about their seas and the lands which were islanded in these seas or lay along their edges.

For them the great rivers counted as part of the sea, the Swan's Road, and so they felt at home with them. That is how you find Norse settlements far from any salt water in Russia, and deep in France and England. The long serpents could find their way right up the Seine, the Thames or the Humber. And it was the same in the Mediterranean. Whether they came first in peace or in war, once they had made up their minds to settle down they made a good job of it. They put as much skill and common sense and forethought into their farming as they did into their sea-faring. But often they kept the old way of inheritance, by which the elder son gets the ship and the younger son the less interesting land. And once they had settled they were slow to move on again. Many modern Danish farmhouses are still on the same site where their bronze age forebears lived, and the farmers are doing fundamentally the same thing – making a living out of the soil – although their tools and methods and crops are so different. Yet even these differences are mostly in the last two centuries, as with farming everywhere.

Up to quite recently Iceland changed less than most European countries, and the Faeroes least of all. Iceland was held back for two reasons.

One was that the climate got worse during the Middle Ages. For six centuries or so cereals could not be grown, although kale has always done fairly well; it became harder and harder for people to make any kind of a living; the level of culture dropped. The other reason was that so long as Iceland belonged to Denmark, there was a tendency for the Danish traders and officials to make money and get into positions of power at the expense of the Icelanders, who were deliberately kept down at a rather low level of prosperity. But, by agreement with Denmark, Iceland is now an independent country and the Icelanders are trying out some interesting schemes, including the municipal ownership of trawlers. For Icelandic prosperity depends on fish – the descendants of the fish that Floki and Faxe and their friends saw in Faxe's Bay. A lot of the fish that we eat in fish and chips comes from Icelandic waters, though some of it is caught by our own trawlers. The Icelanders are now closing Faxe's Bay to foreigners, partly in the interests of fish preservation and partly in the interest of their own fishing industry. The Icelanders are also beginning to replant trees. There were trees of a kind, probably rather stunted birch and pine, when the first settlers came. But they were cut for boat and house building and for fuel, natural regeneration was probably stopped by sheep, and it is only lately that proper forestry methods have been tried. The hot springs are used for heating enormous greenhouses, mostly, I believe, filled with enormous carnations.

Yet, if you go to Iceland today, you will see cereal crops ripening successfully. The climate is changing, quite rapidly, in the direction of tenth-century conditions. This thousand-year swing is rather short and surprising. We do not quite know the causes, but it is clear that great quantities of warm 'Gulf Stream' water is pouring over the ocean shelf between Iceland and the Faeroes and Shetlands, changing the whole marine ecology and, after the sea, the land. Already the northern herring shoals seem to be moving hundreds of miles nearer the North Pole; this may make things very difficult for the western Icelandic herring processing industry. We do not know yet what the Scottish herrings are going to do, but they may move north too – in which case we may have to learn new fishing methods on other types of fish which might move north. That has already happened on the coast of Nova Scotia. Fisheries are opening up along the Greenland coasts, though so far these are relatively uncharted and very dangerous. In another few generations Greenland may be growing some type of vernalised crop. But that is in the future.

There is no thriving Norse settlement in Greenland today. The settlements there came to an end some four centuries after they were founded, and the end seems probably to have been an unhappy one which nobody knew about until quite lately. Even at the beginning of the nineteenth century, Scandinavian missionaries and explorers were still hoping that they might yet come on the old colonies. But during the last twenty years the story of the end of the Greenlanders has been put together, mostly by the Danish archaeologists who dug up the bodies from the churchyard at Heriolfsness (see the end of Chapter XII), and this is what they say.

For a time things went well in Greenland, though it was always a hard life, liable to get suddenly worse if there was a bad year – if it was a very late spring so that the beasts could not get out to the grazing, if any kind of epidemic attacked the sheep or cattle or if the hunters and fishers came back with less than they had hoped from their expeditions. Neither prayers nor sorcery could do much against the hard facts of existence, though they might put courage into the people who had to cope with them, and both were used. A great deal depended on imports of corn, meal and timber. Probably the colonists soon cut down the small birch trees and junipers, and though there was some good driftwood to be found, there was never enough for what was needed. It was used for boat-building, house timbers and panelling – even if the main walls were stone and turf – all furniture, and probably part of the fuel, though they may have done a good deal of turf-cutting. And another thing they had to have was metal, iron and bronze for knives, axes, spearheads, spades and so on. They made do whenever possible with materials like bone and antler, and most of their cooking-pots, drinking-bowls and household utensils in general, were made of soapstone. But any pottery had to be imported, and, of course, any extras in the way of food, especially sweetening of any kind, including wine. They could not even brew beer without corn, though they did try to make wine out of their own sour crowberries.

European stomachs need some bread or porridge, even if, like the Icelanders and Greenlanders, they live quite a lot on milk products. sour milk, cheese and butter. The Greenlanders tried to grow corn, Sometimes their barley – hardiest of European cereals – might just ripen. But it could never be a success, though nowadays it might be possible to grow some of the types of corn which have been made to succeed north of the Arctic circle inside the U.S.S.R.

But they managed fairly well with their sheep and cattle, though it must have been difficult sometimes to keep them alive all winter. And there was plenty of hunting. They got their imports in exchange for furs and walrus ivory, mostly. And they had enough money and energy to spare to build churches and even a small nunnery and monastery, where perhaps their own sagas were written down. Sometimes, no doubt, a Greenlander would go over to Iceland or Norway and bring back stories of the great world, new clothes or weapons – probably something useful! – in exchange perhaps for seal, caribou or fox-skins, or a carved soap-stone bowl made in the long nights at home. They would hear of wars and plagues and discoveries, of the Popes of Rome and the Crusades; but it would all seem very far away.

And the ships came every summer from Norway, or almost every summer. It would be a bad year for Greenland when there had been no sail sighted by the end of the season. And perhaps an occasional ship would come from England, where the adventurers of Bristol were beginning to sail far and wide, or from the Hansa ports in Germany. These voyagers were beginning to develop something like the modern sailing ship, faster and bigger and more efficient than the round-ships which still sailed from Bergen and the Scandinavian ports. But foreign ships were soon forbidden to land by trading agreements with Norway, for the Norwegians were determined to keep the Greenland and Iceland trade.

As the years went on, the trading position grew worse and worse. It ended up as a Norwegian royal monopoly. Only the king's ship, the *Greenland Knarr*, was allowed to trade, and there was an official from Norway sent out to Greenland to see that this was enforced. But some years the ship never came. Perhaps, as the Mediterranean countries settled down to trade with North Africa and elephant ivory became cheaper, there was less demand for walrus ivory. There was less demand for furs too, partly because more were coming in from north Russia, without the expense of a long sea voyage, and partly because of the good woollen cloth made in England and the low countries which was more comfortable and practical stuff to wear, and much cheaper than anything but the roughest fur. Finally, in fact, the Norwegians made up their minds that it was not worth going on with the Greenland trade.

For a time the Church authorities tried to keep up communications. But they might appoint a Bishop of Gardar – that was where the bishop's house and the little cathedral stood – and it could be quite another thing to get him out to Greenland! Only the most devoted cared enough, for at the best it was a dangerous voyage; there was more than a chance of shipwreck and death in the jagged teeth of the ice belt. In the mid-fourteenth century the *Greenland Knarr* was wrecked, and after that there was no more regular communication with Norway.

It seems also that there was a change for the worse in the climate, just as there was in Iceland and Labrador. It seems as though the polar ice cap became permanent, and the Arctic cold spread southwards, until by the seventeenth century the glaciers had come creeping down and everything froze up, including the churchyard at Heriolfsness where the bodies which had been buried in soil with growing plants in it, now stayed solidly frozen for centuries. Now as the Arctic waters warm up, the glaciers are retreating again – how far and for how long? There is a correspondence between storms and sun-spots, but the whole science of climate is still full of rival theories. We might perhaps draw a tentative moral conclusion, that the human race is better – more fully human – in a climate with variation, so that there is always something to react against, to bring out ingenuity and courage. But this must be in the direction of storm and heavy rainfall or snowfall; we wither in droughts – so far, at any rate. But perhaps new ingenuities will be called out from the splendid many-sidedness of mankind.

There is evidence, from pollen analysis – pollen appears to last for thousands of years – that once there was a plague of caterpillars in Greenland. Suppose they ate most of the vegetation in even one year, that would be fatal. Once the cattle and sheep were dead, there would be no milk foods, and already there was little or no cereal food. Think of a small herd where the bull dies one winter of semi-starvation, though every effort had been made to keep him alive enough to be lifted to his feet when the late spring came at last. Any surviving cows would drop their calves. How eager the whole settlement would be for a bull calf! If there were only heifer calves, then they would be the last calves there would be and after that autumn the last milk.

It looks as if the Heriolfsness skeletons provide evidence of this type of under-nutrition, though there is some doubt about it. It was first thought that all the people had been underfed or fed for a long time on the wrong food – they still had plenty of meat and fish, that is, if they were strong enough to hunt and fish – and they were all under-sized, with spine and bone disease and rickets. But, since the first discoveries, archaeologists are less certain that this is so. What is certain is that they were wearing a version of north European country clothes, including jelly-bag hoods, home-spun, a century or so out of fashion.

It was in the increasingly disastrous fourteenth century that the Eskimoes, the Skraelings and trolls, the enemies whom they had never tried to understand or make friends with, began to come down from the north, following the spreading cold and their own ways of ice-hunting. First there would be casual meetings, or avoidings, then there would be a fight. The Eskimoes would begin to know that there were things worth having inside the farms. They might be beaten off the first time and the second, but they would come back, a winter terror, and always more of them and less easily frightened by the settlers, who, each time, might lose a few of their metal pointed arrows or spears. It looks as though in time they had attacked the western settlement and driven out or killed the Norsemen. There may have been a little inter-marrying, but not much. Some of all this comes into the old Eskimoes' stories, but it is all a long time ago, in the days of magic. For many years, until the whalers and such came in the eighteenth century, the Eskimo forgot the white men altogether. Greenland was theirs.

But did any of the Norse Greenlanders escape? Did they go back to beautiful Vinland after time had gone by and the ghosts were laid? It seems that may have happened. In 1347 it is told in the Icelandic annals that a small Greenland boat with seventeen men on board had arrived at Snaefellsness, having been to Markland. On the way home they had been caught by gales and driven to Iceland. There is no astonishment expressed that they had been to Markland. It may have happened fairly often.

One other thing must be borne in mind; a little over fifty years ago a stone slab with a long runic inscription was found by a Swedish farmer in Minnesota. He said it had been under the roots of an ancient tree. This, the Kensington stone, may have been a fake; it was on the whole the age of fakes. But if so it was done by a scholar who knew a great deal about it. Other evidence may turn up, and if so we may need to think of the Norse explorers going inland through the great waterways, perhaps through Lake Winnipeg and the Red River Country. It is possible that men and women went to Vinland and lived there successfully and happily, just as in the nineteenth and early twentieth centuries thousands of later Norse travellers crossed the Atlantic with their families and belongings, settled and did very well, but still keep a Scandinavian culture and outlook in their towns and districts.

Norway, Sweden and Denmark are what people called small countries. And yet when one goes there one has an uneasy feeling of being in a higher level of civilisation than the British one, certainly than the

American one. Even their geographical position has helped them to keep clear of certain aspects of European despair and chaos. Capitalism there has not got into its classical state of contradictions; democracy seems to be working; they are a generation ahead of us in forestry, agriculture and co-operation. And at the back of it all is the courage and solidarity that brought Norway and Denmark through a hideous Nazi occupation, leaving them at the end with enough stories of day-to-day heroism and endurance to make a body of sagas for another generation to look to for confidence and inspiration. They are our cousins. And that is something that both sides of the family know.

BIBLIOGRAPHY

The pleasure of writing this book has been the constant necessity for reading the sagas. Once one starts it is very hard to stop, even though they are really nothing to do with what one had supposed oneself to be looking for. Many of them refer to the same person, but the story is a little different, just as a story told in one village is different from the same story told in the next. I have tried to keep to a more or less consistent spelling which looks reasonable to the eye. Yet we cannot even be sure whether we know how the names were pronounced at the time.

The main general book on this period is, of course, Kendrick's *History of the Vikings*, but I would also hope that anyone who is interested will read Lethbridge's vivid *Herdsmen and Hermits*. I would particularly like to thank Mr Lethbridge for answering a number of my questions – but he must not be held responsible for the mistakes which I shall inevitably have made! At the same time I would like to thank other historians and archaeologists who have helped me, both here and in Denmark.

For the earlier chapters and to some extent throughout the book I have used the *Cambridge Mediaeval History*, Volumes II, III and IV, and dipped into many of the books mentioned in the bibliographies. Also the *Heimskringla Saga,* in translation: *Danish History* by Saxo Grammaticus, in translation: and *Scandinavian Archaeology*, by Shetelig, Falk and Gordon. Throughout the book too I have checked with Nansen's fascinating book, *In Northern Mists*.

In Chapter I, I used Gavin Bone's *Beowulf in Modern Verse*. In several chapters I have used the *Orkneyinga Saga*. This is a Dasent translation. In general his translations are extremely readable and seem to keep most of the original quality; his translation of the *Saga of Burnt Njal* is one of the most exciting books in the world. Volume 3 of Dasent's translation of *Icelandic Sagas* has the saga of Heming in it, and several others as well as the Latin Services of Saint Magnus. I also used Professor Childe's *Scotland Before the Scots* and Ritchie's *Animal Life in Scotland*. Chapter VII is based on the *Saga of the Faroe Islanders*.

For Chapters VI, VIII and IX, and the last four chapters, I used *Origines Islandicae*, translated by Vigfusson and Powell. For Chapter IX I also used *The Chronicles of Novgorod*, translated by Michell and Forbes. Before writing the last four chapters I read *Norse Discoverers of America* by Gaythorne Hardy, *Voyages of the Norsemen to America* by William Hoygaard: *Leif Eriksson, Discoverer of America*, by Edward F. Grey and *Viking Settlers in Greenland* by Norlund.

Almost everybody who reads the sagas get profoundly moved by them, and if they are writers it comes out in turn in their writing. There is Joseph O'Neill's *Wind from the North*, an exceptionally good novel about the Vikings in Ireland, and Linklater's *Men of Ness*. Both these writers are racially part of the people they are writing about; and that means something. It is less obvious why Longfellow's Poems, based on the Heimskringla, are still potent to move one's excitement.

Yet perhaps more important than books is having done so many of the same things that the Norse raiders and settlers did. My farming has been not unlike theirs. I too have sown my corn in small fields by hand and hand-sheared my sheep; I have netted fish as they did; I have felt some of the tide races of the west Highland coast twisting the boat I was trying to steer. I have listened at night for ghosts. And, though our west Highland feuds never quite got as far as murder, that is, after all, only a matter of custom.

51